The Second Book of
Corfu Walks
The Road to Old Corfu

Hilary Whitton Paipeti

HERMES Press & Production

First published 1995

Second Edition ◆ Revised and Updated 1999

Published by HERMES Press & Production, Corfu. Tel. 0661 34496

Printed by Spectrum - Corfu

Original print for cover design by Theresa Nicholas

ISBN 960-85964-2-4

Acknowledgments

Theresa Nicholas for showing me so many walks, and for her cover design; David and Moira Baker for their hospitality in Rou; Hans Vermunt and Henk van der Does for their help with the Mountainbike Tours; my parents for the boots and my brother for the rucksack; Ann Nash for information on flowers; Professor Augustus Sordinas for information on threshing floors; and all the people who showed me the way.

The walker who sets out to discover the countryside of Corfu soon finds that the island offers far more than sun and sea. Just a few minutes from bustling resorts you reach a different Corfu, an island of extensive olive groves, lush meadows or wild mountain crags.

The walker, much more so than the petrol-driven traveller, is in touch with the landscape and its people. The walker encounters the real Corfu, where old women still lead their goats to pasture, where the olive harvest is still a way of life, where old men still sip thick coffee in the dimly-lit coffee bars in village squares.

Corfu is steeped in history and tradition, and the walker can become part of it.

There is no season in Corfu when walking is not a pleasure. Winter can be wet, but there are many sunny days, dry and cold, when the air is clear enough to see over half the island. The warmer days of February, when the first flowers begin their display, beckon the walker with the promise of Spring.

Then Spring burgeons in a flash, and the best season begins, the season when days lengthen and the countryside· is carpeted with flowers. And in the Summer heat, walking takes you into cooler zones, into the shade of olive trees or the breezy hills.

And Autumn is a second spring.

Enjoy the countryside of Corfu, leave nothing but footprints, and take nothing with you but the best memories.

CONTENTS

WALKS

MOUNTAINBIKE TOURS

USING THIS BOOK

MAPS are diagrammatical and, because no Ordnance Survey-type maps of Corfu are available, they were drawn mainly using sketches made whilst walking. They do not necessarily replicate scale, features and alignments as encountered on the ground. Major landmarks on the route are shown, but details may have been omitted, especially on maps which cover a large area. My aim was to help the walker, therefore complex sections of the route may have been drawn to appear larger in proportion to simpler ones. North has been indicated only as a general guide to the orientation of the entire walk, but those with a compass may find that the indicated direction may not correspond with every part of the route.

SYMBOLS

Major trunk road	▦▦▦▦▦▦▦▦▦▦▦
Asphalt road	▬▬▬▬▬
Track (may be passable for motor vehicles)	− − − − − − −
Footpath	− − − − − −
Church	▪ Ch
Building	▪
Ruin	▫
River	〜〜〜
Stream bed (may be dry in summer)	〜〜〜

NUMBERS on the maps correspond with the numbers in the text and are intended to facilitate reference between map and text.

RED OR YELLOW MARKERS have been painted at certain points on some of the walks (indicated in the text). These are mainly to reassure walkers that they are on the correct route. They have been kept to a minimum so as not to cause visual pollution to the environment, and are not intended as a substitute to proper use of the text and the maps.

DURATION figures are based on experience, but have been extended to cover slower walkers and to include rest-stops (but not prolonged ones!).

TIMES must still be regarded as highly variable. For example, one particular walk which I complete in around three and a half hours took five with a slower friend, and seven and a half when on one occasion I accompanied a large group! If walking in the evening, check on sunset time, and note that darkness falls quickly after sundown.

ASCENT is the sum in metres of all significant gradients on the walk, but does not include undulations. Coupled with the parallel notes on terrain, this figure is therefore a helpful indication of the difficulty of the walk.

AMENITIES in villages mostly consist of traditional local coffee bars, which serve alcoholic and soft drinks as well as coffee, and also act as the village store. Sometimes they also provide a snack; we often ask them to open a few tins from the shelves, such as sardines and luncheon meat, and to cut a piece of cheese and a few slices of bread. Most will be glad to oblige.

All walks can be completed by a reasonably active person, unless specified otherwise. Some easier strolls, and shortcuts of longer walks, have also been described for the less dedicated walker who nevertheless wishes to enjoy the island's scenery.

TRANSPORT

Rent a car or take a bus. I have only given precise bus timetables on routes which do not change throughout the year. On tourist routes times change throughout the summer and I have indicated as far as I am able the frequency of the service. Ask for exact times at the information desks at the main bus stations, and be sure to note the time of the last bus back. To travel on blue buses you must buy tickets for both your outgoing and incoming journeys in advance. These are available at the information kiosk in San Rocco Square.

EQUIPMENT AND SAFETY

Corfu's mild climate means that walkers require no special equipment or expensive hiking gear. However, lightweight WALKING BOOTS with ankle support are essential for all mountain walks. Ordinary closed shoes or trainers are suitable for some walks where indicated. Lightweight LONG TROUSERS are recommended, as vegetation can be thorny. Scratches on bare legs running with perspiration cause painfully stinging itches. Clothing is best worn in layers so you can take it off as the day grows warmer. A HAT is highly recommended. If walking during the winter hunting season, wear something brightly coloured so trigger-happy hunters do not mistake you for game.

For your comfort and safety, carry a small RUCKSACK with a WATERPROOF and a SPARE PULLOVER (especially in spring and autumn when the weather is more unsettled). In summer, carry a LONG-SLEEVED SHIRT for protection against the sun. Always have plenty of BOTTLED WATER. If you wish to carry EMERGENCY FOOD SUPPLIES, sesame seed bars, halvas or dried fruit offer a more practical solution than chocolate bars in hot weather!

Also pack a small MEDICAL KIT comprising insect repellent, cream for bites and stings, sunscreen, plasters and elastic bandages.

Don't forget to take a PLASTIC BAG for your litter. Also pack a WHISTLE and a TORCH to attract notice if you have an accident.

It is recommended that you do not walk alone, and that you always leave a written message to say where you have gone. On mountain walks, turn back if the weather looks in the least threatening; it can change very quickly.

If bitten by a snake, don't panic. Corfu's only poisonous snake, the Sand Viper, has a relatively slow-acting venom which affects the respiratory system and a normal adult with no serious allergies should with hospital treatment experience no ill effects. In such an event, tourniquet the limb and get to the hospital as soon as possible, without rushing and without panic, as this will cause the poison to act more quickly. Death from the venom of this snake is very rarely fatal; more people die of bee stings.

CORFIOT COUNTRY CODE

DO NOT LIGHT A FIRE for any reason whatsoever. Thoroughly extinguish any cigarettes and matches and carefully dispose of them. Many of the fires which devastate the island every year are caused by carelessly thrown cigarettes.

DO NOT LEAVE LITTER and especially not broken glass, as this can also cause fires.

TRY NOT TO WALK on the nets laid under olive trees. They tear easily and are expensive to replace. If the net is laid across the path and stepping on it is unavoidable, tread carefully and try not to crush the olives underfoot.

DO NOT PICK fruit or vegetables in cultivated areas. You may be picking someone's lunch. Blackberries are excepted.

DO NOT UNTIE tethered animals. They have been secured by their owner, who will return to collect them later.

LEAVE ALL GATES as you found them.

DO NOT DRINK from streams and wells, however clean they look. Many are polluted with fertilisers and other agricultural chemicals.

RESPECT THE PRIVACY of the local people. Stick to the path and do not wander onto private property or cultivated areas.

DO NOT MAKE A NOISE during siesta hours, from two o'clock to five o'clock. Go quietly through villages.

SPEAK TO THE PEOPLE you meet. The most useful greeting is *Hairete* (be happy), which has three syllables with the stress on the first; the *H* is pronounced as in the Scottish *loch*. Outside the resorts, any attempt made to speak Greek is often met with a response quite out of proportion to the effort put in.

DO NOT PICK wild flowers. Leave them for others to enjoy.

FOOT-NOTE

The tempo of progress still quickens. During the fourteen years since I began to explore Corfu on foot, the island has firmly embraced the modern age and shed all but the vestiges of an ancient way of life.

We cannot prevent, and we have no right to restrict, the desire of the local people to reap the rewards of their prosperity. But since these rewards include new and larger houses, better access to land and property, more shops, more factories, so every year sees development spread to another unspoilt corner, sees concrete obliterate another field, sees new roads scar another wild valley.

I checked all walks personally during the three months prior to publication, and subsequent changes due to bulldozing of new routes or closure of old ones are out of my control. When choosing the walks, I tried to avoid areas where new construction was encroaching, but development erupts in the most unlikely spots, and it is not always possible to guess where the next rash will attack.

There is little doubt that by the time you use this book, some of the routes in it will no longer exist as described. Greece has received huge European Union funding for new roads, and the discovery that what on your last walk along it had been a perfectly good footpath is now a muddy road going nowhere must sometimes provoke the thought that it was bulldozed for no other purpose than to use up spare cash. At the time of writing, a new budget for the 'upgrading' of agricultural access had been ratified, and this comes at the same time as a ban on aerial crop spraying of olive trees is forcing farmers to spray from the ground, thus encouraging demand for road construction. Both factors are certain to precipitate new changes fast.

As a result of the above and other influences, some of my favourite footpaths have recently vanished under the march of progress. I especially regret the ruination of the old path between Katavolos and Rou, bordered in Spring with giant orchids like so many lamp-posts. But wherever an old way has gone, I have discovered an alternative, and often even better route, as between these two hamlets (Walk 21).

The book does not claim to contain all the walks it is possible to enjoy on the island of Corfu. I was limited not only by time but by a self-imposed rule to include only circular walks (with one or two exceptions), and those in areas away from burgeoning development. However, I believe that the walks I present offer both the holidaymaker and the permanent resident the opportunity to explore the varied countryside of Corfu.

Enjoy your journey into the most beautiful island in Greece.

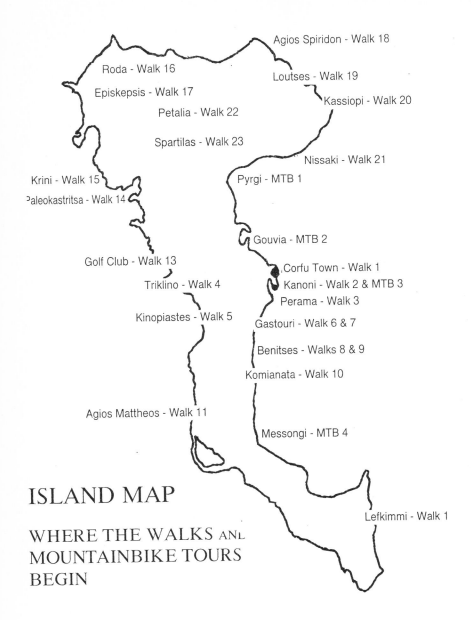

Agios Spiridon - Walk 18

Roda - Walk 16

Loutses - Walk 19

Episkepsis - Walk 17

Kassiopi - Walk 20

Petalia - Walk 22

Spartilas - Walk 23

Nissaki - Walk 21

Krini - Walk 15

Pyrgi - MTB 1

Paleokastritsa - Walk 14

Gouvia - MTB 2

Golf Club - Walk 13

Corfu Town - Walk 1

Triklino - Walk 4

Kanoni - Walk 2 & MTB 3

Perama - Walk 3

Kinopiastes - Walk 5

Gastouri - Walk 6 & 7

Benitses - Walks 8 & 9

Komianata - Walk 10

Agios Mattheos - Walk 11

Messongi - MTB 4

ISLAND MAP

WHERE THE WALKS ANᴅ MOUNTAINBIKE TOURS BEGIN

Lefkimmi - Walk 1

WALK 1   Corfu Town

FORTRESSES AND FORTIFICATIONS

This walk is an exploration of Corfu Town which takes you far from the busy shopping streets, and into the town which the Corfiots know - the Jewel of the Mediterranean. The route follows, more or less, the line of the old town walls, and you will encounter much of their remains. You can also take the opportunity to visit Corfu Town's two splendid fortresses, with their colossal walls and fine views. There is no map, as maps of Town are available.

START San Rocco Square in Corfu Town, if travelling by bus. If you are in a car, it is best to park on the Garitsa Seafront (free) near the Douglas Obelisk and walk up Alexandras Avenue.

DURATION 1 to 2 hours for the walk alone, but allow all day to enjoy the sights fully.

ASCENT Steep climbs inside the two fortresses.

TERRAIN Mainly pavement. Some paths inside the two fortresses.

SHADE Depends on which side of the street you walk!

VIEWS Best view of Corfu Town from the summit of the Old Fortress. Also good views of the port from the New Fortress.

SIGHTS Main ones are the New Fortress, the Old Town, the Byzantine Art Museum, the Palace of Saint Michael and Saint George, the Old Fortress and the Archaeological Museum; but the whole route is one long sightseer's paradise! (Museums close at 3pm.)

AMENITIES All along the route.

EQUIPMENT Ordinary low-heeled, comfortable shoes.

From San Rocco Square, start out along G. Theotoki Street, which departs from the square at the Ionian Bank. Take the first street left, go right at the top, then enter the open market, close under the walls of the New Fortress.

Head up between the market stalls, then when the way bends right, ascend a set of stone steps on the left, between stalls. From the top of the steps there is a fine view of the fortress walls. Here go sharp right and follow the road. Look for a carved stone Venetian lion set into the fortress wall opposite.

The road you are on comes to a stop and you clamber down a short drop to another road where you go straight on downhill between the main fortress wall and the outlying defences. Note another lion, dated 1728, on your right. You reach the sea near the New Port. Here turn right and follow the seafront, where fishing boats moor opposite ships chandlers and other small stores.

Soon you reach the square of the Old Port and, keeping to the pavement you are on, pass the main gate of the New Fortress, which is topped by another Venetian Lion and ringed by a little park. Straight on, you enter Spilia Square.

Proceed across the square and turn right into Solomos Street. The church of Tenedos, with its dome and squat belfrey, is on the right as the street climbs a flight of steps cobbled with flint. At the top of the steps you reach the foot of the fortress walls again, with the fortress entrance on your right A. Just beside the entrance there is a tunnel, and if you wish to cut the walk short here, it leads you through the walls to the top end of the market and then back to your starting point.

If you are continuing, leave the fortress gate and follow the wall around the corner into Schulembourg Street. Below on the left is the old Jewish quarter of the town.

Leave Schulembourg Street by a flight of steps on the left just as the wall ends; at the foot, turn left into Velissariou Street. A short distance down the street, a building with arched doors is the synagogue. Velissariou Street leads you back into Spilia Square, where you immediately turn right, then take the next street left. Ahead of you is the Spilia Gate, which you pass through to emerge into the Old Port Square, where you turn right.

Following the pavement, you pass two narrow streets on the right, then turn right at the third corner into a wide, sloping square with steps which lead up to the Orthodox Cathedral of Corfu B. Approach its facade and then turn left. You reach another small square, where you go straight on and then follow the signs to the Venetian Well, which is up some steps on the left. The 17th century well and eponymous restaurant are located in a picturesque square.

A. The New Fortress, construction of which was begun in 1576 and finished in 1588, was built by the Venetians to complete their work on the defences of Corfu Town. Designed by the Italian Francisco Ferdinand Vitelli, the New Fortress with its underground tunnels and battlements is the most spectacular monument on the island. Its peak is dominated by the citadel, built later by the British in 1843.

B. As you reach the front of the Cathedral, the building on the right displays a plaque which states that it was the first seat of the Ionian Academy, founded by the philhellene Frederick North, Earl of Guilford in the autumn of 1823.

Leave the square at the opposite end to your entry point, at the far corner of the church. You take the first alley on the left, then immediately go right into an open space with a circular railed garden. Turn left here into a wide street with a linear garden and descending steps. At the foot of the steps, you turn right and regain the seafront above the Old Port.

Cross the road, where you can take a flight of steps which descend to the quayside. Straight ahead is the island of Vidos and to the left is the New Fortress. Continue by taking the road uphill along the top of the seawall. Among the buildings you pass on the right are the Solomos Museum C, the Byzantine Art Museum D (housed in a restored church at the top of some steps), the church of Agios Andreas and, just before a sharp right hand bend, the headquarters of the Orthodox Bishopric of Corfu and Paxos.

On the bend, you can descend a ramp and, passing through Saint Nicholas Gate, reach Faliraki, where there is a restaurant, a seafront bar and a small conference centre.

Return to the road and proceed, passing the back of the Palace one the left and the Reading Society E on the right, and then descending into the main square, the Esplanade F. The Liston with its many coffee bars is ahead.

Continue along the front of the Palace of Saint Michael and Saint George G. After the Palace, where the road bends right, there is the picturesque church of Mandrakina. Here leave the road and, at the rear of the church, descend some steps into the moat of the Old Fortress, where fishing boats are moored and maintained.

Walk along the bank of the moat and leave it by taking the steep ascending steps which lead up from under the bridge to the gate of the Old Fortress, open to visitors H.

C. The great Greek poet Dionysios Solomos, who wrote the words of the Greek National Anthem, lived in the house which now contains the Solomos Museum. It contains a collection of memorabilia, archives, and photographs relating to the poet's life and work.

D. Housed in the restored Church of Antivouniotissa, the Byzantine Art Museum contains a priceless collection of Byzantine icons, many of them by Corfu painters.

E Founded in 1836, the Reading Society is the oldest cultural organisation in Greece and contains a fine collection of old books, documents, prints etc., much of relevance to the Ionian Islands.

F The Esplanade Square was created as a result of an attack by the Turks in 1537. The population of the Old Fortress (see next page) had spilled out into the area around the gates, and the commander, fearing that the Turks would use their houses as a stronghold for their assault, ordered their destruction. Part of this large open space was used by the British, during their Protectorate of the Ionian Islands (1814-1864), as a cricket ground. Cricket matches between the five local teams and visiting sides are still played on the ground on summer afternoons. The arches of the Liston, with its coffee bars overlooking the cricket pitch, were built by the French during their administration of 1807-1814.

Leaving the Old Fortress, cross the road and enter the park on the other side of the road. Go left, passing the Monument to the Union of the Seven Islands with Greece - a modern structure with bronze reliefs displaying the symbols of the islands - the Bandstand and the Maitland Rotonda to reach a road. Cross to the garden opposite, where a statue of John Kapodistrias, first Prime Minister of Greece, surveys the fortress. On the right of the little garden, you start to descend to the sea by way of a wide flight of steps, which leads down to the front of the Corfu Palace Hotel. You are now outside the old town walls, and a well preserved section encloses the lovely rear garden of the hotel, where the bar and restaurant are open to the public. After the hotel, take the first street on the right. The second building on your right is the Archaeological Museum, home of the stunning Gorgon Pediment and other antiquities.

Continue along this street (sections of the old wall are visible between the apartment blocks on the right) to a main road, where you turn right, then take the second turn left, uphill. As you turn, you can see on the left a long section of the old wall.

Proceed up the slope to a bend, where on the left cars are parked on top of a bastion overlooking the Prefecture and the Theatre.

Continue by following the road, which enters an open space, with the neo-classical facade of the Ionian Parliament Building on the right. Here take the downhill road to the left, which curves alongside the wall. When it meets a crossing street turn right and then left, then straight on to San Rocco Square.

G. The Palace of Saint Michael and Saint George was built as the residence of the High Commissioner of British Protectorate of the Ionian Islands. Designed by the engineer and architect Sir George Whitmore, its style is neo-classical. Construction began in 1819 and was completed in 1823. The Palace is built of Maltese marble, and until 1864, when the Ionian islands were ceded to Greece, it was the seat of the Ionian Senate, whereafter it became the residence of the Greek royal family. You can visit the State Rooms in the main part of the building, and the east wing contains three art galleries and a bar.

H. In 550 the Goths completely razed the ancient city of Corcyra, which was located near Kanoni. The surviving Corcyrans decided not to rebuild their ruined city, but established themselves instead on the headland which we call today the Old Fortress. On this rock, with its natural defences, they built a new town using materials taken from the walls of the ancient city. The major part of the fortresses man-made defences were added under the Venetians, beginning in 1550. Apart from the defences themselves, the buildings which exist in the fortress were added by the British for military use, and some of these have been restored. Exhibitions featuring historical and religious aspects of the island run during summer.

WALK 2   Kanoni and Environs

A JOURNEY THROUGH THE HISTORY OF CORFU

Close to town, and passing through its busiest suburbs, this walk nevertheless seems to touch the countryside. On the route, you take a trip through the whole history of Corfu, with sights ranging from Ancient Greek remains to memorials of last century's British Protectorate.

START San Rocco Square in Corfu Town, if travelling by bus. If you are in a car, it is best to park on the Garitsa Seafront (free) near the Douglas Obelisk and start and finish the walk at 8.

DURATION A good half day to enjoy the sights in full.

ASCENT 150 metres.

TERRAIN Mostly on asphalt and pavement. Some paths and tracks.

SHADE Variable.

VIEWS From Agia Marina, the highest point of Kanoni.

AMENITIES Bars and restaurants are plentiful. See recommendations in the guide.

EQUIPMENT Comfortable shoes.

Start by taking the street leading out of the south-west corner of San Rocco Square (Donatou Dimoulitsa Street). Soon you pass a wing of the Psychiatric Hospital on the right, where stretches of old wall are part of a bastion which protected access to the main town gate. Then you reach a five-pointed crossroads (1) where you take the narrow road opposite. The British Cemetery A is a short distance along this road, on the left.

After the Cemetery, continue along the road to reach the prison B, where you turn left and follow the road alongside the wall, with a pine forest on the other side. At the rear of the prison, take a road sharp left and go downhill to meet a street at 2 (Kiprou Street C), where you turn right.

A. A place of immense interest both to historians and to botanists, the British Cemetery is a peaceful oasis close to the busy town centre. No-one can fail to be moved by the inscriptions on the headstones, which date from the British Protectorate (1814-1864) to the present day. The cemetery is famed for its trees and flowers, especially for the wild orchids, which in spring bloom everywhere.

B. The Penitentiary of Corfu was built during the British Protectorate and today is still in use. At the time of its construction, it was the most modern prison in Europe, the first to provide individual cells instead of crowding inmates into communal facilities.

Map - WALK 2

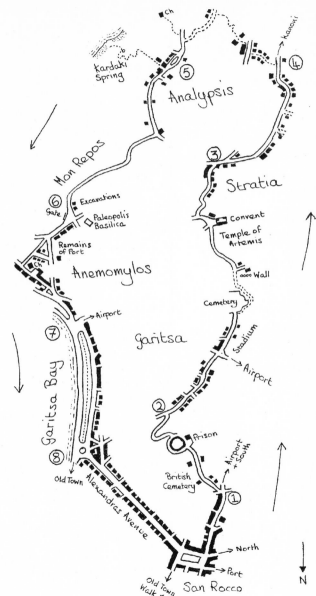

Keep going until you reach a major crossroads (the sports stadium is opposite on the right) where you cross straight over and continue to the gate of the main town cemetery. At the gate, where the road ends, take an asphalt path to the right which runs alongside the wall. The path becomes a track which, at the back gate of the cemetery, leaves the wall and heads up a slope. At the top of the slope, note on the right the section of old wall D.

After this wall, the track becomes asphalt. Soon you pass on the right the site of the ancient Temple of Artemis E and then the Convent of Agios Theodoros the Tiro F.

After the convent door, you take the next road to the right, which leads uphill through the houses of Stratia to join the main Kanoni road at 3. Turn right here and then, taking care of traffic, fork right onto the one-way circuit (traffic comes from behind). There are several fine but decaying Belle Epoque houses here.

The road leads through a countrified part of Kanoni, with only a sprinkling of houses. Proceed for some distance to where the road twists through a cluster of buildings. About a hundred metres after the houses, at 4, look on the left for a concrete path which takes you up to join the upper section of the one-way circuit.

Here turn right and at the far corner of a block of buildings on the left of the road ascend a partially stepped path to meet a track. Here go left and proceed to a road, where you go right. Then take a sandy footpath, which leaves the road on the left and runs uphill to the church of Agia Marina, situated on the highest point of the Kanoni peninsula with splendid views both towards the sea and over Lake Halikiopoulos and the airport.

C. Shortly after you start along Kiprou Street, look on the left for a small stone column. An inscription on the column informs us that the street was 'made by the prisoners of the penitentiary in the year 1854'.

D. The wall is the only remaining section of the wall of the ancient city of Corcyra, and dates from the 5th century BC. This section escaped destruction because a chapel was built against it in the 12th century.

E. The Temple of Artemis, whose extensive remains you see on the right of the road, was one of the most important temples of the ancient city of Corcyra. Built in the 6th century during the Doric period, it was a huge, many-columned structure measuring about 47 metres by 20 metres. The famous Gorgon Pediment, which is housed in the Archaeological Museum, was discovered here in 1812

F. In the 5th century AD, an early Christian basilica was built next to the temple, probably using stones taken from the earlier building. Its proximity to the ancient remains shows how the early Christians used pagan temples to site their own churches, in order to facilitate the conversion of the local people. The nave and southern aisle of this church still exist in the more recent church of the convent, which is dedicated to Agios Theodoros the Tiro, a 5th century martyr. An inscription on the door lintel informs us that the convent was given to the nuns in 1816 by Sir Thomas Maitland, first British Lord High Commissioner.

Return down the sandy footpath to the road again, where you go right and soon reach a small roundabout (5), where you start off down the main road. Just as you pass the roundabout, take an alley on the right, which becomes a path down steep steps and alongside the wall of the Mon Repos estate, and you eventually reach Kardaki Spring G. Another short and rough descent brings you to a shingle cove.

Return up the steps to the roundabout and turn right. The road runs downhill, following the Mon Repos wall; at a junction, go right and continue alongside the wall down a leafy lane to a crossroads (6).

At the crossroads H, turn right past the main gate of Mon Repos I (visit the estate and villa on a separate walk), and at the next fork go left. The excavations you pass on your left are part of the ancient harbour, behind which the market place began. Then take the first road right, after which you go left. Ahead, on the left, is the Church of Saint Jason and Sosipatros J. At the T-junction, go left.

Presently the street reaches an open space in front of the main gate of the church. Continue to follow the street to just before its junction with a main road. Before you reach this road, take a wide alley to the right, which leads past an old church built on the walls of the ancient harbour, onto a road.

Cross the road and enter the park on the other side, then go left, following the park to a major road junction (7). Cross the road and continue through the linear park which backs the seafront, where paved paths lead beneath eucalyptus trees and amongst exotic shrubs and cactus plants.

G. The Spring of Kardaki, its water flowing from the mouth of a Venetian lion, is reputed never to run dry. An inscription on the spring says that those who drink from it will never again see the shores of their homeland. A sign indicates that the water is now unfit to drink.

H. At this crossroads, on the left, you can see the covered archaeological remains of a late-Roman bath house and villa. Excavations have determined that the site was occupied from Ancient Greek times up until the 6th century AD, when the ancient city of Corcyra was abandoned. The bath house formed part of an extensive complex of entertainment facilities which adjoined the market place and harbour area.

More excavations are underway in the field on the other side of the road, where segments of what appears to be an integrated pavement have been discovered at diverse locations in the area, leading archaeologists to theorize that the marketplace of the city of Corcyra was the largest in the ancient world.

The ruin facing you is the Palaiopolis Basilica, the oldest church still standing in Corfu. It was founded by Jovian, a 5th century bishop, and was constructed using materials taken from nearby older buildings. Ancient columns and capitals can still be seen in its structure. Its history is one of destruction and rebuilding over the centuries, but it was finally damaged beyond repair in the last war.

Continue through the park until it stops at a roundabout (8) with a stone column in the centre (The Douglas Obelisk, dedicated to General Sir Howard Douglas, British Lord High Commissioner from 1835 to 1841).

Here go left, crossing (with care) the road and taking a street leading away from the sea (Menekrates Street; the British Consulate is on the corner).

This street soon reaches a six-pointed crossroads, where you head straight on and slightly left. A few metres along this road on the right, you will see the Tomb of Menecrates K, in the garden of the police station.

Return to the crossroads and take the second street on the left. You then reach the tree-lined Alexandras Avenue, where you go left and proceed back to your starting point in San Rocco Square.

I. Still at the crossroads, on your right, more or less opposite the Basilica, is the gate of the Mon Repos estate. In the grounds stands an elegant villa in Regency style, which was built in 1831 as summer residence for the British Lord High Commissioner. It subsequently became the summer home of the former Greek Royal Family. Ownership of the estate is at present a subject of dispute between the former King Constantine and the Municipality of Corfu. The park is open to the public, and its wide paths make it a delightful spot for a stroll amongst the majestic trees. At the far end of the park is a small and very well preserved Doric temple, probably dedicated to Poseidon and dating from around 500 BC.

J. The church of Saints Jason and Sosipatros is one of only two typically Byzantine churches on the island and dates from the 10th or 11th century. The saints were bishops and disciples of Saint Paul, and brought the religion to Corfu around 70 AD.

K. The Tomb of Menecrates is a circular cenotaph dating from around 600 BC, and was discovered in 1843. Menecrates was a citizen of Oianthia on the Corinthian Gulf and was a great friend to the Corcyrans when the island was vying with Corinth for naval supremacy. After he died in a shipwreck, the Corcyrans erected this monument in appreciation of his ambassadorial services. So says the archaic inscription which runs around the base of the monument.

Map - WALK 3

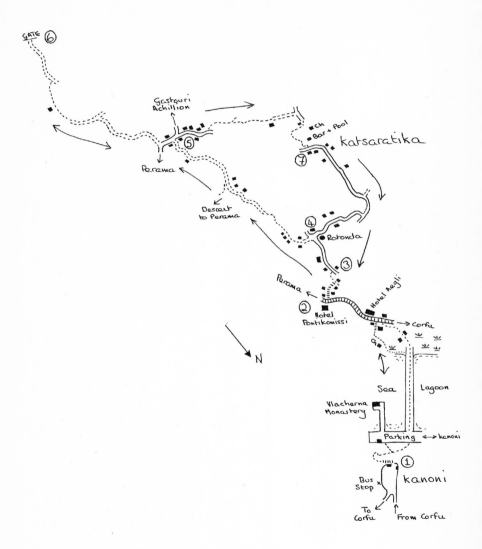

WALK 3   Perama and the *Yarda*

IN THE STEPS OF BRITISH ENGINEERS

The British-built water system (see Walk 8) which supplied Corfu Town is the theme of this stroll. Some of the route follows the access path used by the engineers; because it was one yard wide, it came to be known as the 'yarda'. This is also 'Durrell Country', made famous by Gerald Durrell's 'My Family and Other Animals'.

START At the turnaround point at Kanoni.

GETTING THERE

By bus: Bus no. 2 Kanoni, every half hour from the Esplanade Square, and from bus stops on Alexandras Avenue (blue bus). The terminal is your starting point.

By car: Follow signs. Fork right before ascending to Kanoni viewpoint and park (small charge) by the Vlacherna Monastery.

DURATION 2 to 3 hours.

ASCENT 200 metres in several small stages.

TERRAIN Mainly roads and tracks.

SHADE Mostly in shade.

VIEWS Fine view of Lake Halikiopoulos and airport from Villa Vigiris. Famous view from your starting point at Kanoni.

SIGHTS Remains of British-built water aqueduct and works buildings. Vlacherna Monastery and Mouse island (ferry service from Vlacherna).

AMENITIES Bars at Perama (descend by footpath as marked) and at Katsaratika.

SWIMMING At Villa Vigiris pool (no charge, but you should buy a drink).

EQUIPMENT Ordinary closed shoes.

Start at 1 beside the café which faces the viewpoint, where a flight of steps leads down to the coast. Where the steps divide, you can take either way to reach the sea near Vlacherna Monastery. Then cross to the other side of the lagoon via the causeway, reaching the road at Perama.

Here turn left and continue as far as the swimming pool of the Pontokonissi Hotel (2). Caution: the road is busy. Keep in single file and well into the side. Opposite the pool, you see a flight of steps. Ascend them, then at the top go left to a road (3), where you turn left again.

After a short climb you reach a junction (4) beside a rotonda, part of the old waterworks buildings. At this junction, turn left along a track which very soon becomes a path, and later a track again, running through olive groves above Perama. You pass more evidence of the water system, including a miniature aqueduct dated 1840. Finally, you meet a road near a junction (5), where you turn left downhill.

Very soon the road bends sharp left and at this point you take a track going right. The track, sometimes narrowing to a path, runs through olive groves and forest, then reaches a track. Turn left here and after a short walk you descend and reach a gate (6). The gate, if it is closed, denies access to the spectacular 14-span aqueduct which crosses the gully; however, you can glimpse the structure through the citrus trees.

The walk returns from this point to 5, where this time you take the road straight on, signposted Katsaratika. Just after the first huddle of buildings, take a footpath to the left. Go right where the path forks, whereafter you reach a villa, and the path becomes a road. At the next junction, go right and after the track bends right, take a path straight on between fences. This path meets a road at 7, and on your immediate left you find the gate of Villa Vigiris, where you may use the pool and bar, and enjoy the view from the pool terrace (open in high summer only).

Leaving the path, or the Vigiris garden, turn left and follow the road. After a descent, you reach the rotonda again at 4, from where you return to Kanoni by the same route, not forgetting to take the descending steps at 3.

If you would like to know more about the life of the Durrell family in Corfu, as portrayed in 'My Family and Other Animals' and 'Propero's Cell', look out for 'In the Footsteps of Lawrence Durrell and Gerald Durrell in Corfu (1935-39)', a guidebook which charts the locations described in their books. Available in bookstores in Corfu and at selected bookshops in England.

WALK 4   Kombitsi and the Pine Woods

MYSTERIOUS FOREST

One of the natural wonders of Corfu, the Kombitsi woods are just a few minutes drive from Corfu Town yet easily missed by all but hunters. Comprising a huge area of woodland between Kombitsi and Kalafationes, the main feature is the great number of Pinus pinea, the Stone or Umbrella Pine. The canopy of this beautiful tree, close planted, forms cushions of bright green on hillsides and in dales. It is a region of mystery and silence, where you will feel almost like a pioneer.

START At the Varipatades road junction near Triklino.

GETTING THERE

By bus: Bus no. 11 Pelekas. Hourly or every two hours from San Rocco Square (blue bus).

By car: The starting point is six kilometres out of Corfu Town, on the Pelekas road. Park by the main road.

DURATION 2 to 3 hours.

ASCENT 200 metres, with the steepest section up to Bastouni.

TERRAIN Forest tracks and some asphalt roads.

SHADE Plenty in forest, but some walking in full sun.

VIEWS Good view of Corfu Town and suburbs from Bastouni.

SIGHTS The Venetian Spring at Kombitsi.

AMENITIES Traditional coffee bar at Kombitsi.

PICNIC In any forest clearing (please be especially careful to not cause a fire).

EQUIPMENT Ordinary strong closed shoes, except in winter when it may be muddy.

Follow the road towards Varipatades until you reach, after a hundred metres or so, a carpentry workshop. Leave the road opposite and head for an electricity metre, on the other side of the river bed. Passing left of the metre, head up a bank (where brambles may block a clear way through) and then bear right, heading along and diagonally across a flat area. Reaching its far side, you bear left and ascend a forested hill on a narrow and partially overgrown footpath. CAUTION: The route was overgrown at the time of writing; don't give up.

At the top of the ascent, where the way is clearer, follow the track to the left alongside a chain-link fence, then through forest again. Keep to the main track, then go left when you meet asphalt, proceeding to the centre of Kombitsi (2), where an old building, formerly a monastery, and a church stand at a crossroads.

Map - WALK 4

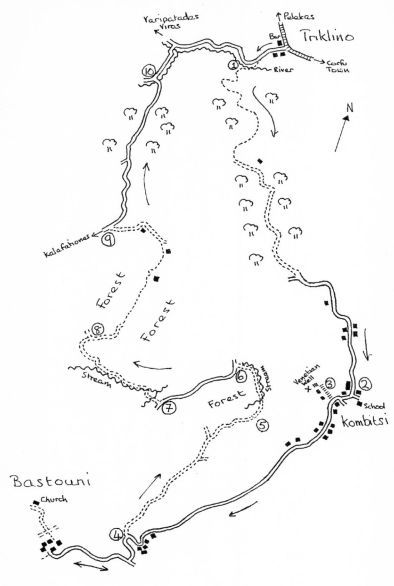

Go right and after a few metres right again. You will now see a wide, cobbled path leading straight downhill (3). This path leads past a restored Venetian house and into a courtyard with cisterns and a spring, all dating from the 18th century. Return to the road at 3 and turn right.

Proceed along the road (passing point 4 on the map), and go right at the next junction, continuing uphill until you reach the forecourt of some houses. Here go up the forecourt, and take the alleyway between houses. Emerging at the back of the hamlet, head straight on up a steep track which ascends to a church, with a small graveyard, a radio mast and a wide view of Corfu Town and its periphery. Return to 4.

To continue, take the track which leads off the road at 4. It gently descends a flat-bottomed, narrowing valley, then plunges into the forest (5). Keep right at a major fork. The track descends to the stream bed and follows its course, so the route may be muddy in winter, and even impassable after heavy rain. Continue to meet a wider track and turn left.

Proceed to a clear track on the right (7), with a hut visible through the trees. Take this track past the hut and ascend to a division of the way (8). Here you go right and follow the path past two fenced huts and on through the forest. Keep going to meet a gravel and dirt road at 9, and go right.

At the next major T-junction, where the road crosses a river bed (10), turn right. A short walk on and you reach the Triklino-Varipatades road, where a right turn and a walk of a few minutes will return you to your starting point.

Map - WALK 5

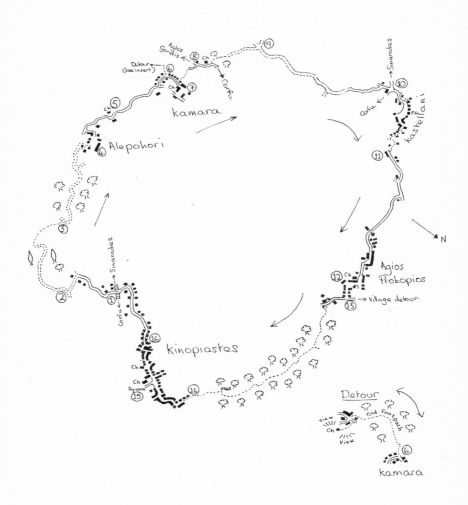

WALK 5   Kinopiastes - Kastellani - Agios Prokopios

PICTURESQUE VILLAGES

A delightful exploration of several of the picturesque and traditional villages of the central, or Messis, region of the island. The walk mostly takes you into the villages by the back ways, and gives you a glimpse into the real life of Corfu.

START On the main road to Sinarades, at the Kinopiastes turn-off (Tzerà).

GETTING THERE

By bus: No 5, almost hourly from Methodios Street near San Rocco Square. On the hour from Town, on the half hour to return. Ask to get off at Tzerà.

By car: Take the main road south and go straight on at Vrioni. Keep straight on to reach the Kinopiastes turn-off. Park close into the side at the wide junction.

DURATION 3 to 5 hours, depending on detours.

ASCENT 150 metres, mostly in a steep climb at the start.

TERRAIN Tracks, paths and minor roads.

SHADE Shady through the olive groves.

VIEWS Pleasant, if not spectacular, vista from Agii Theodoroi.

SIGHTS A very well preserved section of ancient cobbled footpath.

AMENITIES Traditional coffee bars in most of the villages. Restaurants (evening only) in Kinopiastes. Tripa is recommended, with set menu including wine and entertainment.

EQUIPMENT Strong, comfortable shoes.

Begin the walk at 1 by taking the narrow road which leaves the main road opposite the road into the village of Kinopiastes (that is, on the same side as the petrol station). After bridging a river bed, this road soon heads uphill sharply, then levels out and continues as a track to join another track (2).

Here turn right and continue uphill. The track eventually becomes a path, wet and muddy underfoot after prolonged rain, and after a further climb, meets at 3 a track (good views over cypress tree-tops towards Corfu Town).

Turn right downhill and follow the track for some distance until you reach habitation - Alepohori (Village of the Foxes). Immediately before the first building which directly abuts the track, leave the track by a path which leads you into the village square at 4 (no facilities).

Turn left and follow the road, which exits the square and swings left around the houses and then goes right. Look back here; the village has almost a fortified appearance. You now follow the road, passing a renovated water source and an old church at 5, until it reaches the next habitation, which is Kamara.

Passing the first few houses of the village, you take the first road left, which is surfaced with concrete and heads between some houses until it meets a junction (6). At this point, the walk continues to the right, but an optional detour is recommended.

DETOUR: turn left at 6 to follow a cobbled path which ascends through olive groves. This path is a remaining section of the old donkey road to the south of the island - the 'M1' - and its surface is in a remarkable state of preservation. It is registered by the Archaeological Department, and we hope that pressure to bulldoze it to make a motor road can be resisted. The path eventually emerges onto a road at a junction. Here turn left, and crossing the road in front of you, take a set of steps which leads you to a little church and graveyard. There is a fine view from here towards Corfu Town, and at the rear of the churchyard you can glimpse the sea on the west coast at Agios Gordis. Return down the old path to point 6.

Continuing the walk at the junction where you began the detour (6), carry straight on (If you did not take the detour, you will have turned right) and follow the alleyway, past some picturesque cottages on the left, into the village square (7) where you will find a small bar for refreshments.

Corfu's villages were once joined by a network of cobbled footpaths, and the path between Kamara and Agii Theodoroi was one of the main routes to the south. These beautifully made paths are certainly as old as the villages they connect, and were constructed using the stone available in the vicinity. But motor transport has replaced donkeys - and feet - as a means of getting around, and even paths which have not been bulldozed for new roads are becoming overgrown due to lack of use. And no-one with the skill or the time is left to repair damage by winter rain, resulting in the gradual decay of one of the great and unappreciated treasures of Corfu, as important in their way as any fortress or palace.

Other walks which in places follow inter-village paths with some cobbled sections still intact are 7, 8, 9, 10, 14, 15, 16, 20, 21 and 23.

To continue the walk from 7, return up the alleyway, taking the first path on the right, which is surfaced in concrete with shallow steps. It leads downhill, crosses a stream bed and heads up the other side of the gully, where it meets a track. Continue straight on to reach a main road (8).

Here turn right, and very soon you will pass a walled churchyard, after which look on your left for a path (just before the bend in the road), which you now follow. A little further on, the path becomes a track.

At the next junction of tracks (9), turn right and follow the track through a cultivated valley. Heading uphill and now metalled, the road joins an access road to a church and then reaches a crossroads at 10.

Go straight on, crossing the main road with care, then into the village of Kastellani Messis. Entering the village, note a fine house on the left. Pass through the village 'square' (little more than a widening of the street, but with a post office and some bars), and follow the road as it goes sharply left.

After the bend, look on the right for some steps down off the road (green rails protect the drop), and take this path between houses. Turn left at a T-junction of paths and keep going until you reach a road (11).

Here turn left and then take the first asphalt road on the right. A short walk, and you reach the first part of the village of Agios Prokopios, where the road runs between terraces of houses painted in shades of coral, sienna and strawberry. Continue to a second group of buildings, where on the right a large church adjoins the road (12).

Just after this church, turn right to follow a street which emerges onto a narrow road bordered on the far side by green rails (13). Here you may turn left to make a detour (not described or illustrated - don't get lost) to explore the picturesque village and take refreshment. Or turn right to continue the walk.

From point 13, proceed past the last house, where from the top of a holding wall (more green rails) you can view Corfu Town and the mountains of the mainland. Immediately at the end of the railings, you see a path heading downwards to the left, beginning with some rough asphalt steps. Follow this path, initially between low walls, then winding down through the olive terraces. Although the path is narrow, the way is reasonably clear.

Passing a stone well-head, then a hand-pump, at point 14 the path runs into an alleyway at the outskirts of Kinopiastes. Follow the long alley to a road, whereupon you go right to reach the main village square at 15 (several traditional bars here; a perfect setting to conclude the walk. Note that bars are not always open during winter).

To continue, proceed through the square, and as the road take a right-angle bend to the right after the church (note marble carving around the door), head straight on along an alley paved with beige stones. At a little square in front of another church, take the left hand alley and when it reaches a T-junction, go left, then take the next turn right, around the back of the chapel, to reach the main village road again at 16.

Here go left to regain, after a few minutes walk, your starting point at 1.

WALK 6   Mount Agia Kyriaki

IN THE FOOTSTEPS OF SISSI

This short walk takes you in the footsteps of the Empress Elizabeth of Austria (Sissi). You visit the palace she built, pass the well-head she bestowed on the village, see the view she enjoyed and the chapel where she prayed and found peace, and stroll through the village where she strolled.

START At Gastouri, at the gate of the Achillion Palace. Use the map for Walk 7.

GETTING THERE

By bus: Bus No. 10 Gastouri - Achillion 07.00, 10.00, 12.00, 14.15, 17.00, 20.00 from Methodiou Street near San Rocco Square (blue bus).

By car: Take the main road south and go straight on at Vrioni; follow signs to Gastouri and the Achillion Palace.

DURATION 2 hours (not including Achillion visit).

ASCENT 200 metres, steep to Agia Kyriaki summit.

TERRAIN Tracks and stony footpaths.

SHADE Mainly shady.

VIEWS Spectacular vista from Agia Kyriaki summit.

SIGHTS Achillion Palace, Sissi's Spring.

AMENITIES Bars and restaurants in Gastouri.

EQUIPMENT Strong, comfortable shoes.

Start at 1, at the gate of the Achillion Palace (fee for admission). Take the road towards Gastouri village, proceeding as far as 2, where amongst a group of houses a church stands beside the road on the left.

Here leave the road by an alleyway beside the long building on the left just after the church (the way is indicated by a blue and yellow sign reading ΠΡΟΣ ΙΕΡΟΝ ΝΑΟ Υ.Θ. ΟΔΗΓΗΤΡΙΑΣ) which descends between cottages. Take the left hand way at a fork and you will reach a road, where contemporary frescoes of the Achillion Palace decorate the arcades of the building opposite.

Turn right and on the next corner (3) turn left along another alley, which is paved with beige stones and again is indicated by the blue and yellow sign. This alley leads directly to the church which is the subject of the sign, where you can rest in its wide courtyard with benches (4). On the right just as you enter the yard is the 'Cultural Centre'. The building is usually kept closed, but contains the installations of an old olive press, which can be made out through the windows.

To continue, leave the courtyard by steps at the corner. When the steps meet an alley *, you turn right and follow the concrete path through a gully (spoilt by dumping of waste) to where the concrete path surface runs out. Here go left to ascend a wide alley between houses and onto a road.

Turn right and proceed a short distance, until in the shade of two massive plane trees you reach 'Sissi's Spring'. Continue on about 70 metres to a bend and take a path which heads off left (5). For much of its length surfaced with rough cobbles, the path sometimes deviates from its old route, especially in its upper reaches, but it is not difficult to pick up the way again.

Eventually, it climbs onto an extensive olive terrace, where a clear way is lost. Here head for a hut ahead, climb up the terrace wall and continue across the next level to hit a road (6), where you turn right and continue to ascend.

Proceed to where power lines cross the road. A few steps on, there is a clear dip in the road and here, at 7, the path to the summit leads off right. After a sharp climb up mossy steps you reach the church at the peak, where the view encompasses a large part of the central section of the island.

Return to the gravel road at 7 and turn back the way you came. Now follow the road back to Gastouri, where you reach the village at a crossroads (8). To complete the walk, turn right and a short walk returns you to your starting point at the Achillion Palace.

* If you wish to cut the walk short at this point, turn left and the alley will take you back to the frescoed building.

Perhaps the most complete example of the direction of classicism in all of Greece is Corfu's famous Achillion Palace. It was built for the Empress Elizabeth of Austria on this site in Gastouri, which was bought from the widow of the philosopher Petros Vraïla-Armenis, and it was here that the Empress lived her last years. After Sissi was assassinated, the Palace was purchased by Kaiser Wihelm II of Germany, who spent happy summer holidays here until the outbreak of the Great War. If the architectural style is eclectic, in the way of the last years of the 19th century, the sculptures that adorn it are entirely in the classical spirit. Especially celebrated are the statues of the Muses, as well as the two statues of Achilles, 'Mortal Achilles' by Ernst Herter, and 'Achilles Triumphant' by Johannes Gotz.

WALK 7   Achillion - Mount Agia Kyriaki - San Stefano

PILGRIMS' PATHS TO AGIA KYRIAKI

Explore a quaint village, visit one of Corfu's most famous sights, enjoy one of the best views on the island, and return along an ancient footpath.

START At the Achillion Palace in Gastouri.

GETTING THERE

By bus: Bus No. 10 Gastouri - Achillion 07.00, 10.00, 12.00, 14.15, 17.00, 20.00 from Methodiou Street near San Rocco Square (blue bus).

By car: Take the main road south and go straight on at Vrioni; follow signs to Gastouri and the Achillion Palace.

DURATION 2 to 3 hours, without Achillion visit and swimming.

ASCENT 300 metres, steep to Agia Kyriaki summit.

TERRAIN Some tracks and roads, but also steep and stony footpaths.

SHADE Mostly in reasonable shade.

VIEWS Spectacular vista from Agia Kyriaki summit and from above San Stefano.

SIGHTS Achillion Palace, Kaiser Bridge.

SWIMMING At Kaiser Bridge.

AMENITIES Coffee bars and restaurants in Gastouri. Pool bar at the San Stefano Hotel.

PICNIC On the rocks above the San Stefano Hotel.

EQUIPMENT Strong, comfortable shoes. Swimming gear.

Start at 1, at the gate of the Achillion Palace (fee for admission). Take the road towards Gastouri village, proceeding as far as 2, where amongst a group of houses a church stands beside the road on the left.

Here leave the road by an alleyway beside the long building on the left just after the church (the way is indicated by a blue and yellow sign reading ΠΡΟΣ ΙΕΡΟΝ ΝΑΟ Υ.Θ. ΟΔΗΓΗΤΡΙΑΣ) which descends between cottages. Take the left hand way at a fork and you will reach a road, where contemporary frescoes of the Achillion Palace decorate the arcades of the building opposite.

Turn right and on the next corner (3) turn left along another alley, which is paved with beige stones and again is indicated by the blue and yellow sign. This alley leads directly to the church which is the subject of the sign, where you can rest in its wide courtyard with benches (4). On the right just as you enter the yard is the 'Cultural Centre'. The building is usually kept closed, but contains the installations of an old olive press, which can be made out through the windows.

Map - WALKS 6 & 7

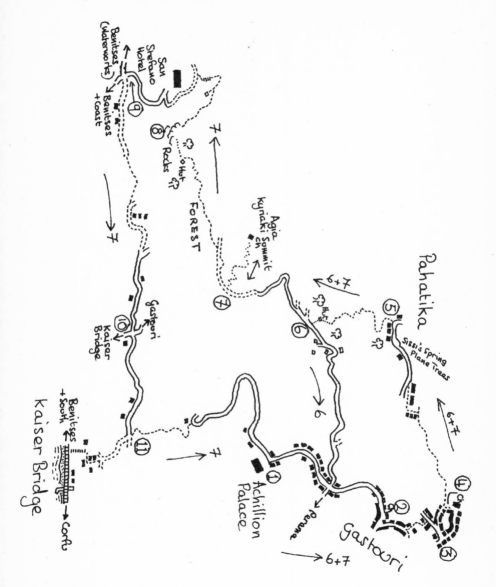

To continue, leave the courtyard by steps at the corner. When the steps meet an alley, you turn right and follow the concrete path through a gully (spoilt by dumping of waste) to where the concrete path surface runs out. Here go left to ascend a wide alley between houses and onto a road.

Turn right and proceed a short distance, until in the shade of two massive plane trees you reach 'Sissi's Spring'. Continue on about 70 metres to a bend and take a path which heads off left (5). For much of its length surfaced with rough cobbles, the path at one point deviates left, and then returns to its old course.

Eventually, it climbs onto an extensive olive terrace, where a clear way is lost. Here head for a hut ahead, climb up the terrace wall and continue across the next level to hit a road (6), where you turn right and continue to ascend.

Proceed to where power lines cross the road. A few steps on, there is a clear dip in the road and here, at 7, the path to the summit leads off right. After a sharp climb up mossy steps you reach the church at the peak, where the view encompasses a large part of the central section of the island.

Return to the gravel road at 7 and go right. Proceed for about 150 metres and turn off on a clear footpath which runs down alongside the high holding wall of an olive grove, then plunges into woodland. Descending sometimes very steeply, the narrow path eventually emerges into an untended olive grove beside a hut which is no more than pieces of old tin tacked to a framework of branches. Ahead, the olive grove falls in shallow terraces, with the sea in the distance. Stand with your back to the hut and turn 45° to your right. This is the direction you must head (if you have a compass, it is south-east). In winter when they are not obscured by vegetation, you see some flat white rocks below you. Make your way down four terrace walls, about 50 metres, to reach the rocks (8), from where all the east coast is in view.

Having admired the spectacular scenery, proceed to the right, and just beyond the last of the rocks you pick up a narrow footpath which leads down through woodland again. At a pump house which supplies water to the San Stefano Hotel, it joins a wider path, which swings to the left and descends some steep and very slippery steps beside the water pipes. You emerge onto a wide track with fire hydrants, where you go left, passing the main building of the Hotel and joining its access road at the children's playground. Keep going downhill to the hotel gate (9).

Immediately after the gate, turn left along a track, which becomes a footpath which passes through a gate and becomes a track again. Further on, it continues as asphalt. Cross a road at 10 and proceed to where the asphalt stops (11). Here take a path to the left, climbing sharply to reach the road. Keep going uphill to reach your starting point at the Achillion Palace.

Detour to Kaiser Bridge

At 11 continue to descend by way of the concrete road. After a brief descent, a path goes right, then reaches the seafront down some steps. There are several bars for refreshment, a beach for swimming and the jetty built for the Kaiser, which gives the little resort its name. If you have travelled by bus, you may return from here to Corfu Town on the No. 6 Blue Bus, whcih passes more or less every 75 minutes. Alternatively, ascend to 11 again to return to the Achillion Palace.

Starting the Walk from Benitses

Start at the harbour square in Benitses and take the road into the old village. Proceed until the road, crossing a bridge, emerges from between the houses into an open space, from where several roads radiate. Take the concrete road on the right, which crosses another bridge and ascends.

Climb to its junction with a track and go right to reach the San Stefano Hotel, where you join the main walk at the hotel gate (9).

In the days before roads, the footpath by which you ascend to Mount Kyriaki, and the descending path to San Stefano, were the routes taken by pilgrims who climbed to the summit on the name-day of the church (July 7). This pilgrimage is described superbly by Neil Macvicar in his book *A Heart's Odyssey* (see bibliography).

Of course, the most famous of Agia Kyriaki's pilgrims was the Empress Elizabeth of Austria (Sissi), in whose footsteps you follow in this walk and the previous shorter one. An inscription in marble embedded in the wall of the church reads: 'In this holy place, the wounded Empress Elizabeth, praying, regained her peace.'

Kaiser Bridge, as its name suggests, was built for the Kaiser and his entourage to embark and disembark on his steam yacht, the Hohenzollern. He then would reach the palace by way of a carriage road winding up through the gardens. The bridge was broken during World War II, and the jetty was restored for the European Summit of 1994.

The proprietors of the San Stefano Hotel have kindly allowed this walk to pass through their grounds. Please respect this concession.

The hotel's swimming pool is the largest and one of the best in Corfu - certainly it has the best view - and is open to the public, the only payment being that the proprietors request that you buy a drink at the pool bar.

WALK 8   Benitses - Stavros - Agii Deka Mount
DONKEY PATHS AROUND THE MOUNTAIN

Almost wholly on the old donkey paths which used to connect the picturesque villages of the region, this route takes you around and over Corfu's second highest mountain, Agii Deka. Highlight is a visit to the abandoned monastery close to the summit, where patches of cultivation form a little oasis, a Shangri-La on the mountain crest. On your return you may visit the British-built waterworks.

START In the harbour square at Benitses.

GETTING THERE

By car: Follow main road south as far as Benitses harbour. Park in designated spots beside the road.

By bus: Bus no. 6 Benitses. Every 75 minutes from San Rocco Square (blue bus).

DURATION 4 to 7 hours.

ASCENT 576 metres.

TERRAIN Cobbled donkey paths and rough footpaths.

SHADE Mostly shady except on the moutain between Ano Garouna and Agii Deka.

VIEWS Superb views from many points on the route.

SIGHTS Abandoned monastery near Agii Deka summit. British-built waterworks behind Benitses (detour from the main walk).

AMENITIES Traditional coffee bars in Stavros, Ano Garouna and Agii Deka.

PICNIC In the monastery grounds on Agii Deka Mountain.

EQUIPMENT Walking boots and long trousers essential.

Set off from 1 by taking the village street opposite the kiosk. Where it divides into three, take the middle way, a flight of shallow steps. At the top, continue straight on, crossing a bridge and then following a path through chicken runs. At the first two junctions of paths take the right hand route and you reach a stretch of level ground with views to the right over the rooftops of Benitses, whereafter you go left at the next two junctions.

At 2 you are now on the old path which ascends from Benitses to Stavros. Keep always to the upward path, going straight across a level patch where a track crosses and continue to ascend through forest, where the path may be overgrown in places.

39

Map - WALK 8

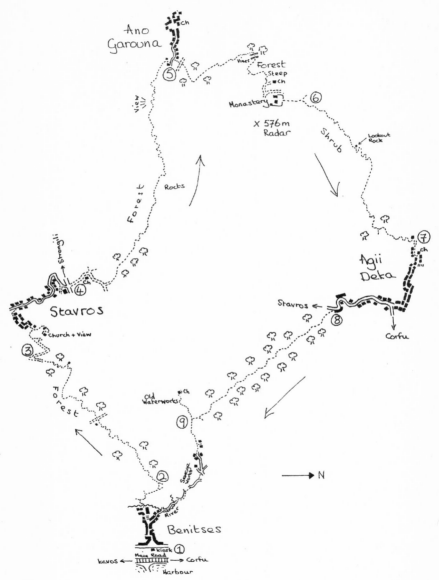

Eventually, the path becomes a track, whereafter you take the first track right (3). You follow this track as it curves uphill, and on the first right hand bend you take a path straight on towards the houses of Stavros. When you meet a crossing path near the houses, turn right to reach, after a short walk, the hilltop church of Stavros, from where there is a splendid view over Benitses and the coast towards Corfu Town.

Return the way you came, this time taking the footpath straight on through the houses, where it winds past picturesque ruins and crosses a little square. Follow the main alley, and you will descend a concrete ramp to the village road. Turn right and follow the road, passing on the right the village bakery with its verandah roof supported by olive trunks, then just after the next bend take a concrete alley left. Head down between the houses (passing a working olive press) to join the road again. Continue downhill briefly, then cut off the next bend on a footpath beside the church. A little way downhill, you reach the main road junction (4).

To continue, cross the road at 4, taking the (so far) unmade road which you see on the other side. After the track bends right at a chapel, and starts to ascend, look for a track leading off to the left beside a cultivated patch. This track soon becomes a path which leads up and down gullies, through a natural fortress of conglomerate limestone in wierd formations, across a rocky hillside with views southwards, then into olive groves near the village of Ano Garouna. The main path is clear; but if in doubt, bear right (except just after the rock formations, when the right hand path leads to a hut).

When the path reaches a concrete road at 5, turn left. (A short walk down this road brings you into the village for refreshments if required). The walk, however, continues about 50 metres after your left turn at 5, when you leave the road by way of a path on the right. Climbing sharply, the path crosses a track and continues steeply up through olive groves, with some level sections where you can catch your breath. It runs by a vineyard, then climbs briefly to an open plateau with more vines, where a clear way is lost. Ahead you see a rocky cliff which is the last obstacle to the summit; you are making for the chapel you can see on the skyline. At this point, cross the vineyard diagonally to the left, and head into the olive grove on the other side. A few steps into the trees, look on the right for a break in the terrace wall. Here the path heads up two terraces, rounds a rock and plunges into a shady tunnel of holly oak trees, circling the back of the vineyard. You go left at a fork and climb very steeply to emerge suddenly onto a cleared area beside the little chapel you could see from below. Follow the track downhill to the walled monastery grounds just below. You can visit the church, restored in 1994.

To continue, leave the monastery grounds by way of the main gate, where a path runs beside an orchard of cherries and walnuts. You reach a junction of paths (6), where you take the right hand one, which after a steep and rough descent, leads to Agii Deka village. Keep always to the downhill path and take care of loose stones.

Eventually, you descend some rough steps to a parking area at 7, where you go right to follow a path beside a wall to reach the gate of a churchyard. Continue along the alley which leads away from the gate as far as an old building with a curved wall, where you take the alley which goes right, and not the steps which lead downhill. When this alley meets another one, turn right and continue to a road. Here go straight on and proceed until, after a double bend, you see a roadside shrine on the right. A few paces on, opposite a little garden strangely named the 'Lovenest', you leave the road by a path on the left (8). This is the old route to Benitses, and some sections of its cobbled surface remain. The path descends, then meets another footpath at 9. Here, a short detour to the right will take you to the British-built Water Springs (see Walk 9).

To complete the walk, at 9 turn left downhill. The path descends some steps, follows a raised walkway and thereafter becomes a road. Keep to the main road as far as a fork where your way down is signposted to 'Benitses Centre'. Descend to cross a bridge, turn left to cross another bridge and head straight on down the village street of Benitses back to your starting point.

WALK 9   Benitses - Stavros - Water Springs

A SECLUDED CHURCH AND THE WATER SPRINGS

You don't have to go far from a busy resort to reach unspoilt countryside, as this ramble in the hinterland of Benitses shows. During the walk, you climb through olive groves to visit two secluded little churches, both a perfect spot for a picnic, then descend by way of the British-built Water Springs.

START At Benitses, in the harbour square.

GETTING THERE

> By bus: Bus no. 6 Benitses. Every 75 minutes from San Rocco Square.
>
> By car: Follow main coast road south to Benitses. Park in designated areas in the harbour square.

DURATION 2 to 3 hours.

ASCENT 300 metres.

TERRAIN Footpaths, some cobbled, and woodland tracks.

SHADE Mainly shady.

VIEWS View of Benitses from Agia Paraskevi. View of coastline from Stavros.

AMENITES Traditional coffee bar in Stavros.

PICNIC Beside either of the two little churches, or at the Water Springs.

EQUIPMENT Strong, comfortable shoes. Trousers recommended.

Start at the newspaper kiosk in the harbour square at Benitses (1). Set off by taking the village street opposite the kiosk. Where it divides into three, take the middle way, a flight of shallow steps. At the top, proceed straight on and cross the river, after which you follow a path between chicken runs. Ignore all paths to the right until you meet an obvious crossing path, where you turn right.

Follow the path, cobbled and climbing gently through olive groves. When you meet a track at 2 go left, then leave the track on the next bend where the path continues up through the rocks to rejoin the track (so far unmade).

Turn left, and after a short walk you will reach the concrete ramp which leads to the little church of Agia Paraskevi (note the fine view of Benitses just before the ramp). At the rear of the church there is a courtyard with permanent tables, where a spring flows under the umbrella-like shade of a giant oak tree.

Map - WALK 9

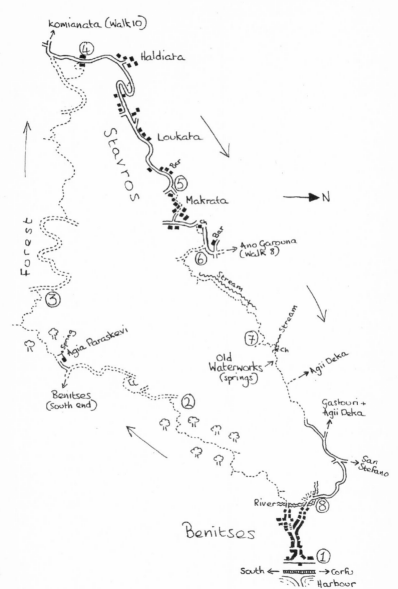

To continue, take the path which runs alongside the courtyard and into olive groves. Keep always right, and then make a sharp ascent to a (so far unmade) road at 3. Here turn right and proceed uphill for ten to fifteen minutes. Leave the road (now asphalt) by way of a stony and rough path on the left, which ascends sharply through olive groves. Just where the way starts heading downhill, the main path goes sharp right, continuing its ascent to a track, where you go right. Turn right off the track just before the houses to take a concrete alley to the road at 4.

(Here a left turn will soon take you to point 2 on Walk 10, from where you can follow the guide to 'explore the mountain ridge', or simply climb to the telecom mast for a fantastic view, a spectacular objective for the walk.)

The main walk continues from 4 with a right turn downhill, and you walk past the hamlets of Haldiata and Loukata (traditional coffee bars here). After Loukata you pass the village bakery with its verandah roof supported by olive trunks, then just after the next bend you take a concrete alley left (5). Head down between the houses (passing a working olive press) to join the road again. Continue downhill briefly, then cut off the next bend on a footpath beside the church. A little way downhill, just before you reach the main road (bar here), take a track right (6).

After a short distance, you turn off the track to the left, on an indistinct footpath beside a hut, running downhill. Keep going downhill, and you enter a valley where the path, following the right side of a stream bed, may be overgrown. After a path joins from the left, the way becomes clearer. Continue to where the path is bordered by a chain-link fence, where you turn off at 7 onto a narrower path to the left (what seems to be the main path peters out later in some olive groves).

This path leads very steeply downhill, crosses the stream bed, and runs to a little church in sight ahead. At the church, go round the front of the building and descend some steps, then follow the path (may be overgrown) beside the waterworks. A tunnel leads to the source of the spring.

To complete the walk, continue on the downhill path. It descends some steps, follows a raised walkway and thereafter becomes a road. Keep to the main road as far as a fork where your way down is signposted to 'Benitses Centre'. Descend to cross a bridge (8), turn left to cross another bridge and head straight on down the village street of Benitses back to your starting point.

The waterworks were constructed by Sir Frederick Adam, the Lord High Commissioner of the British Protectorate from 1824 to 1832. From the waterworks, a great aqueduct was built to carry the water along the coast to Corfu Town, and Walk 3 follows part of this route. Before the construction of the waterworks, the population of Corfu had either obtained their supplies from wells and cisterns in the town, or bought it from market vendors, who had brought it by pack mule from the river near Potamos.

Map - WALK 10

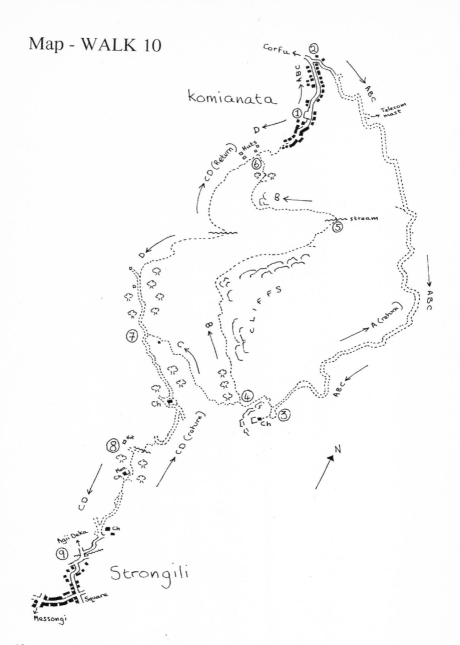

Corfu

② ABC

komianata

ABC

① Telecom mast

D

CD (Return)

Huts

⑥

B

stream ⑤

D

CLIFFS

B

A (return)

⑦

C

ABC

B

④

Ch

③

ABC

Ch

N

⑧ Hut

Mon Ch

CD (return)

CD

Agii Deka

Ch

⑨

Strongili

Square

Messongi

WALK 10   Komianata - Stavros Mountain - Strongili

EXPLORING a MOUNTAIN RIDGE

The long ridge of Stavros Mountain offers a variety of walks which suit every ability. Everyone will enjoy the wonderful panorama, stretching down the southern part of the island.

START At Komianata, where the road ends (all walks).

GETTING THERE

By bus: Stavros: 06.15, 08.30, 12.30, 15.00, 17.00 from Avramiou Street Bus Station (green bus). Get off at the terminal.

By car: Take tha main road south from Town and go straight on at Vrioni. Then continue straight until you fork left for Agii Deka. Pass through Agii Deka, then take next left to Stavros. The walks begin where the road ends. Park by the road just before Komianata, but not in the wide space, where the bus turns round.

DURATION 2 to 4 hours, depending on which combination of routes you use.

ASCENT Walk A: 150 metres, in two sharp climbs. Walk B: 200 metres. Walk C: 350 metres, with steady ascent on return from Strongili. Walk D: 250 metres, with steady ascent on return from Strongili. Note that as Strongili is 250 metres lower than Komianata, the ascent is made on the return journey.

TERRAIN Walk A: Mostly earth track. Walks B and C: Rough and stony footpaths after 3. Do not attempt Walks B and C if you are not prepared for some rough walking. Walk D: Stony footpath and track.

SHADE Walk A and B: No shade. Walk C: No shade to 6. Walk D: Shady through olive groves.

VIEWS Good views from the Pantokrator church near 4.

AMENITIES Coffee bars and shops in Strongili.

PICNIC Walks A, B and C: In the little yard behind the Pantokrator church. Walk C and D: Anywhere in the olive groves.

EQUIPMENT Walk A: Ordinary strong shoes. Walks B and C: strong walking boots and trousers essential. Walk D: Strong walking boots essential.

WALKS A, B AND C: Start at 1 by walking away from Komianata, back in the direction from which you came, and take the first road on the right (2). At first surfaced with concrete, then with gravel and earth (possibly asphalt in the future), the track climbs steeply then levels out to run just under the edge of a long ridge. There are fine views to the right and, when the track begins to descend, an . extensive vista ahead over the whole south of the island.

After dropping steeply, the track ends at the chapel of Pantokrator (3). There is a yard behind the chapel, with benches above the steep drop (take care with children and do not allow them to scramble on the rocks at the edge).

WALK A: Return the same way to your starting point.

WALKS B AND C: From the chapel, return a short distance along the track, looking on the left for a very narrow and steep path leading off it beside a rock. The way is marked with splashes of blue paint. The path drops sharply under a cliff, then veers away from it. Now look for a path going left (4), marked with blue paint. Here Walks B and C diverge.

WALK B: Ignore the path left at 4, continuing straight on along olive terraces. Then the path makes a long, ascending traverse of the shrub-covered hillside, where the way is rough and in parts overgrown. Gradually, it swings into a side gully and continues the traverse along the foot of some cliffs and crags, until it drops off left to cross a stream bed in the gully (5), whereafter you begin to head uphill again. Fork left just before you reach some more olive trees, head straight on through them, then left. Soon the path gives out, but below on your left you see a clear path. Head down to reach this at 6, and turn right for the village of Komianata and your starting point.

WALK C: At the junction of paths at 4, take the path left (marked with splashes of blue paint). The path descends overgrown terraces, then levels out through scrub. Reaching olives groves again, it passes a hut and descends to meet a track at 7, where you turn left for Strongili, now following the instructions for Walk D.

WALK D: Begin at Komianata (1) and head towards the main village. You pass through a tiny sloping square, leaving it by its lower corner on the left, and then follow the alley into meadows outside the village. The scenery is very pretty but is unfortunately ruined by extensive deposits of litter.

Keep to the stony path, which descends steadily to cross a stream bed at then continues to descend into olive groves. Only fragments remain of this path's old cobbled surface, and there are many loose stones. Plunging into the olive groves, the path joins a track, where you keep left. Passing 7, you glimpse the houses of Strongili ahead.

The track then reaches a white-washed church; circuit left around its front. A few steps on the track divides. Here go right and when the track doubles back on itself, take a path left (on the outside of the bend) which proceeds across an olive grove and then turns right along a line of cypress trees.

Then you see a hut ahead (8). Before the hut, turn left and head across the olive grove towards an old church with adjoining ruined monastery buildings, visible through the trees. There may be no clear path here; use the church buildings to get your bearings. Keep the church on your right and follow your nose past it, deviating right at joining tracks (but never heading back in the direction you came), until the way becomes a vague track. Where the track is gated, take a path on the right which skips the blockage.

Follow the track to reach a church, where you continue down a concrete road to join the main road at 9. Turn left here and take the next road left, by which you enter the village of Strongili. The main square, with a tiny shop/bar, marks the centre of the village, and at this point you can turn right to reach the main road again, where there are a couple of bars and a shop, or turn left to make an exploration of the upper part of the village.

Return by the same route to Komianata, taking care not to lose your way where the paths are unclear around the monastery, and being sure to take the upper track beside the church.

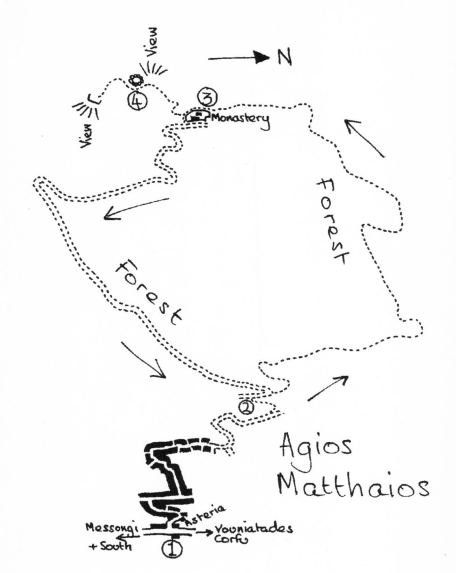

WALK 11   Agios Matthaios Mountain

VIRGIN FOREST

On the slopes of Agios Matthaios Mountain, the primeval woodland which once covered Corfu remains. On this high, conical hill, the scenery resembles Corfu before civilisation, even before mythology.

START At Agios Matthaios Village, at the Asteria Bar.

GETTING THERE

> By bus: Agios Mattheos: 3-4 buses a day from Avramiou Street Bus Station (green bus).
>
> By car: Main road south from town. Go straight on at Vrioni, then follow signs. Park in the indicated village parking.

DURATION 2 to 3 hours.

ASCENT 300 metres.

TERRAIN Path on ascent, unmade road with gravel on descent.

SHADE Shady on ascent, descent mainly unshaded.

VIEWS From the summit and on the descent.

AMENITIES Bars in Agios Matthaios, but none on the route.

PICNIC In the shady grove just below the monastery, where there are wooden picnic tables, or near the survey column.

EQUIPMENT Strong shoes.

Start at the Asteria Bar (1), where a concrete road leads off the main village road. The road doubles back and meets a wide alley, where you turn right. Then you take the first alley on the left, and follow it uphill. Where it meets a rough road continue ascending, then fork left on a rougher track. Very soon you climb to an unmade road at 2, where you go right. You leave this road almost immediately on the first bend to continue up a wide footpath, which ascends steadily through forest. Levelling out near the summit, the path reaches the Pantokrator Monastery in its walled grounds (3), just below the highest point of the mountain.

Reaching the monastery gate, turn right and follow the path alongside the wall. At the far corner, the path leads you straight on away from the wall and climbs, past a little viewpoint, to a topographical survey column set on the wall of a ruined enclosure (4). The hillside drops away steeply to give an almost vertical perspective of the coastline and Lake Korissia far below, and on a clear day Paxos is visible.

Past the survey column, a narrow path continues a short distance through lovely forest to a picnic area perched on a sheer slope, with a dizzying view of Agios Matthaios and the valley beyond.

Return to the monastery wall and go right to reach the wide access track. Your descent from here is down this track to 2, where you head off the track to descend into the village again. Take care not to miss the path; it comes just after an abrupt bend to the right. Alternatively, return by your ascending route.

In ancient times, Corfu was covered with forest, but human interference has removed all but a few woodland areas, such as on the Agios Matthaios mountain and at Kombitsi (Walk 4), where pine woods spread for miles.

In cultivated areas, olive and cypress trees predominate, blanketing the low inland hills and valleys. But where cultivation stops, the land, like in all part of the Mediterranean, has deteriorated into 'maquis', a tangle of aromatic shrubs and bushes with a few low trees. One of the most common shrubs is the kermes oak, which resembles holly, and there is also myrtle, oleander, heather, hawthorn, strawberry tree, honeysuckle and the herbs rosemary, thyme, oregano, sage and bay. In spring, such areas bloom with orchids.

Walks which pass through typical maquis are: 8, 9, 10, 11, 14, 16, 17, 18, 19, 20, 21, 22 & 23.

WALK 12   Lefkimmi - Alikes

RIVER, MARSHLAND AND SALT PANS

Corfu's landscape offers contrasts, and no contrast could be greater than between the bare mountains of the island's north and the fertile flatlands of its south. In this walk, you stroll alongside a wide river whose banks are a riot of flowers in spring; you cross a wilderness of marsh; you reach disused saltpans; and you return through ancient, shady olive groves.

START At the Lefkimmi River Bridge.

GETTING THERE

> By bus: Kavos: every 1-2 hours from Avramiou Street Bus Station (green bus).
>
> By car: Follow the main road south to Lefkimmi.

DURATION 3 hours. Allow one hour for a stroll alongside the river and back.

ASCENT None.

TERRAIN Well made tracks and paths. Not to be attempted in winter or early spring, when the area is often flooded.

SHADE None to 4. Shady through olive groves between 4 and 5.

SIGHTS Interesting derelict industrial landscape at the salt pans.

SWIMMING On coast near 3, and at Bouka Beach on the other side of the river (extra walk or car trip).

AMENITIES Restaurants and bars near the river. The River Restaurant is highly recommended.

PICNIC By the church at 3.

EQUIPMENT Ordinary low-heeled closed shoes will do. Wellingtons required after rain (see note on terrain).

Four roads lead off the main road at the bridge (1) and run along the river banks. Facing south away from Corfu Town, take the one on the left along the north bank, that is, on the same side of the river as Corfu Town. Follow the road almost to the sea, to a little harbour cut into the river bank.

Here on the left a track leaves the road (2). Take this track, which runs between marsh plants then, as an unmade road, converges on the shore. Go straight on to the point where the road suddenly stops (3). A track goes right here to a chapel on a beach. Your way continues straight on, however, as a path which heads for the nearby radar station.

Map - WALK 12

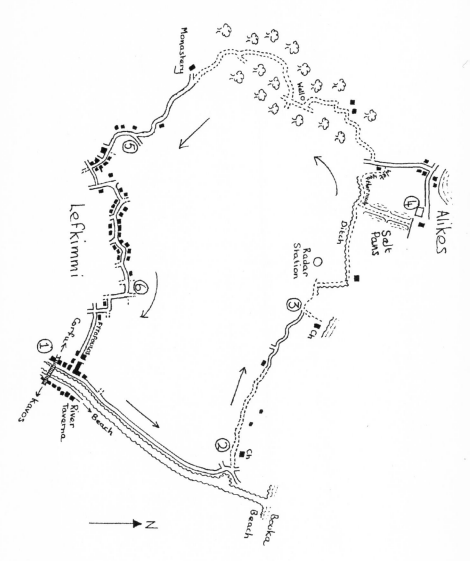

Approaching the station, you meet the corner of a ditch, whereafter you follow a track alongside it, making for an isolated building straight ahead - the old salt works.

When you reach it you cross a ditch (you may need to walk a short distance left, where it narrows, to jump the ditch if it is full) then turn left to follow the path along a low embankment between two ditches. The embankment skirts the salt pans on your right. Proceed to where you see a low causeway; take this across the pans, heading straight for a church and other buildings on the far side. In winter, the water laps at its edges, but the land is baked dry in summer (if the causeway is covered, simply continue along the embankment to meet the road). Reaching the buildings, you bear left and pass the Venetian warehouses (4), built with a mixture of white and pink stone and red and yellow brick, then take the road towards Alikes, where you take the first road left.

Now you take the first clear track on the right, which soon enters olive groves. Follow the main track, with your only deviation being a right turn at a crossroads just after a well. At a monastery with a cemetery, the road becomes asphalt. Bear right where a road joins from the left (5).

Now proceed straight on to a crossroads, where you turn left downhill. Reaching a T-junction, you go left again. A right at the next junction, and you follow the main way as far as FYTOPOULAS ST., which you turn left to follow. This street now heads directly back to the river, and a right turn here brings you back to the bridge where you started.

Recommended: *The River Taverna, which is located on the other side of the river from your starting point. Real Greek home-made cooking; exceptionally good prices; tables on the quayside.*

Map - WALK 13

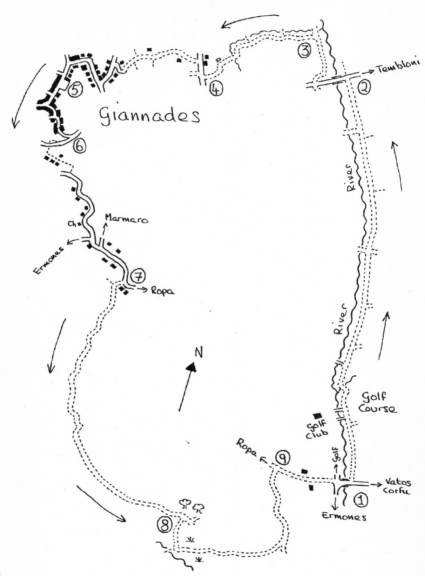

Giannades

Tembloni

River

River

Golf Course

Golf Club

Golf

Ropa

Vatos
Corfu

Ermones

Marmaro

Ch

Ermones

Ropa

N

③

②

④

⑤

⑥

⑦

⑧

⑨

①

WALK 13   Ropa Valley

CORFU'S AGRICULTURAL HEART

Corfu's agriculture is not based solely on the production of olive oil. In the fertile Ropa Plain at the very centre of the island, sheep and cattle graze, and a sea of grass grows tall, green in spring and golden in summer. The walk follows the river which bisects the plain, visits the region's main village, then heads back along a minor valley,where lush fields continue.

START On the Vatos-Ermones road at the gate to the Corfu Golf and Country Club, just where the road crosses the river.

GETTING THERE

By bus: Glyfada-Vatos: 4-5 buses a day from Avramiou Street Bus Station (green bus). CAUTION: Not all Glyfada buses serve Vatos.

By car: Take the Pelekas road out of Corfu Town, then after junction left to Pelakas at 6.5 kilometres, go straight. Then follow signs for Golf Club and Vatos. Park beside the road, or in the Golf Club, if you are going to use the facilities.

DURATION 2 to 3 hours.

ASCENT 100 metres in one short ascent from plain to Giannades.

TERRAIN Mostly paths and tracks. Some road walking. Flatland paths may be muddy after rain.

SHADE Negligible.

VIEWS Good view of Ropa Valley from Giannades.

SIGHTS The lovely plain of Ropa with its teeming birdlife.

AMENITIES Traditional bars and shops at Giannades.

PICNIC Anywhere in the fields, but not on land which has been cultivated.

EQUIPMENT Strong, comfortable shoes.

At the starting point (1), take the road which runs alongside the river on the other side from the Golf Club access road. This road follows the course of the river towards the greens, runs past the club house (reached by pedestrian bridges over the river) and out into the Ropa Valley.

Continue alongside the river for about two miles until at 2 you reach a stone-built road bridge (dated 1903). Cross this bridge, and continue on a track along the opposite river bank, leaving the river when a grassy track heads off left (3). The track improves as it heads towards Giannades village, which you can see on the hill ahead.

When the track meets a road, turn right then take the second track to the left, which ascends gently then steeply to the village. At the village road turn left, then take the first alley right, wide at first, then narrowing between houses (this alley is not illustrated on the map). After a short walk uphill, you reach the village road, where you carry on into the village square at 5, where there is a fine view over the valley.

Continue by proceeding through the square to the point where the road turns quite sharply right, and here take the alley going left. Now you descend to the road by following the main alleyway, and when you reach the road at 6 turn right. A few steps on, leave the road again by a footpath on the right (indistinct), which ducks under the road through a tunnel then heads straight on past some houses and meets the road again, where you turn left.

The walk continues along this road for some distance through agricultural scenery. Go straight on when you come to a junction for Ermones (right) and Marmaro (hard left). After a few more minutes walking, look for a track on the right (7), which leaves the road on the outside of a bend to the left. (If you reach a road signposted 'Ropa' you have gone too far.)

Take this track, which descends gently then follows the edge of the valley floor. The hills on your left are mainly covered with shrub and woodland. As the track fades (8), you swing right across the flat field, where the track is indistinct, heading towards some willow trees.

Soon the track reaches the river bed and gets clearer, running as an unfenced grassy way through the fields. At a junction, keep left, whereafter the track surface improves. When it meets a bumpy road (9), turn right and a short walk brings you back to the gate of the Golf Club and your starting point.

RAMBLES near PALEOKASTRITSA

Paleokastritsa is so pretty that few people venture far from its dramatic coastline. But in its hinterland is a network of donkey paths and tracks which lead the way into a region which is even more beautiful.

START at Paleokastritsa, at the bus terminus and parking area on the beach front.

GETTING THERE

By bus: Paleokastritsa: every 1-2 hours from Avramiou Street Bus Station (green bus).

By car: Follow main road to Paleokastritsa. Park at the seafront, or in designated parking areas.

DURATION Walk A: 2 to 3 hours. Walk B: 4 to 5 hours.

ASCENT Walk A: 250 metres. Walk B: 500 metres.

TERRAIN Cobbled footpaths and tracks. Some asphalt on all walks; take care of traffic.

SHADE Walk A is mainly shady. Little shade on walk B.

VIEWS Spectacular views of Paleokastritsa from the Lakones area, especially on ascending path after 4, and from the summit of Arakli.

AMENITIES Bars in Lakones.

EQUIPMENT Boots with good grip. Trousers essential for Arakli ascent.

From the starting point (1), walk along the road in the direction of Corfu Town, then just after a road goes right to Alipa Bay, take the road on the left. Go left at a fork and thereafter climb until, after a level section, the road makes a sharp bend left (2), 50 metres after power lines cross it.

On the elbow of this bend, take a footpath, which dips under an overhanging rock and crosses a small gully and then continues across olive groves with the land falling away on the right, to meet a wider path beside two huge pine trees. Here turn left to follow the mainly cobbled path which climbs a narrow valley, crosses a track and leads into the village of Lakones, where it meets an alley at 3.

The village square, with its shops and bars, is a few steps to the left, but your route continues to the right and proceed past a church and alongside a wall until the path widens and, just ahead, drops steeply. Here (4) you will see on the left a flight of wide steps leading uphill; these take you up to the main village road.

Map - WALK 14

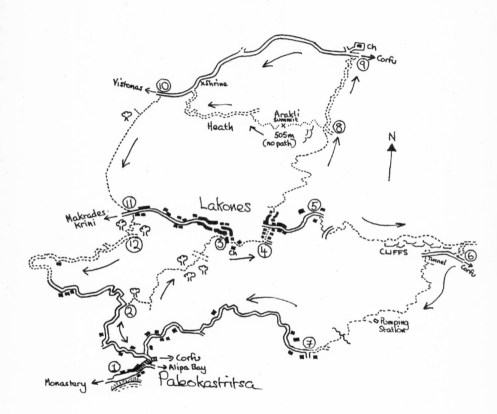

WALK A: Here turn right and follow the road for a little way until on the right you see, just after a concrete drive leads down to a house, a flight of concrete steps (5). These lead down and become a very steep stone footpath, almost a watercourse. Descend with care to meet the road again, cross over and take the continuation of the path, less abrupt now. Though you do not realise it at first, you are walking almost on the edge of the cliff, and this become clear as a magnificent view opens up. Continue to meet a concrete road where you turn right and meet the main Lakones - Paleokastritsa road again at 6. Here turn right, uphill. Some 150 metres up the road, look on the right (the cliff side) where you see a path which leads down and tunnels under the road. You are now almost directly under the viewpoint on the cliff footpath. After the tunnel, where the path divides, turn sharp right and follow the cobbled path as it winds downhill. Reaching a pump house, bear right and keep going downhill. The path crosses a watercourse and meets a grass track, where you go right to reach a narrow road at 7. Here go right and follow the road, which in places ascends briefly, back to your starting point.

WALK B: Cross the main village road and continue up the flight of steps opposite. Where the houses cease and olive groves begin, you meet a crossing path, where you go right. The path, which is cobbled with shallow steps, ascends in a series of switchbacks, leaving Paleokastritsa below in a steeper and steeper perspective. Then it reaches the top of the pass (8) and joins a track coming from the right. At this point, you may make the ascent to Arakli (page 62).

If you are not climbing to the Arakli summit, keep to the descending track. A church in a walled yard is a prominent feature ahead, and you meet the road nearby at 9. Here turn left along the asphalt road (caution; busy in summer). As you proceed, some fine views open on your right, and the bulk of Arakli mountain is on your left. After some distance, you pass a small roadside shrine on your left; approximately 200 metres further, in a portion of cultivated land planted with vines, look on the left for a very narrow footpath (10). The total distance from 8 to this path is 1.4 kilometres.

The path is somewhat overgrown initially, but you persevere and it becomes clearer, with a mainly cobbled surface, running straight down a valley to reach the road at 11.

Here cross the road and take the drive and concrete steps which descend beside a shop which produces olive wood souvenirs. The path descends steeply in sharp zig-zags, then meets a track (12). Go right and continue down the main track, taking care not to slip on the loose gravel, to your starting point.

ARAKLI SUMMIT ALTERNATIVE: *Only attempt this if you are fit, unafraid, prepared to push through thick and spiky bushes, and are wearing strong trousers. There is no path.*

Exactly at the top of the pass immediately after the path joins the track (8), look for an indistinct path on the left, leading into the bushes. Initially the path is clear, but then it fades out and you have to push your way forward. Bear to the right of some rocks and, having passed them, start making your way to the left. The undergrowth gets thicker, but eventually starts to clear as it approaches the horizon. This is a false summit, but the actual peak is now visible ahead, marked by a survey column. The encircling view encompasses Corfu Town, the west coast and the sea beyond, and Angelokastro.

When you decide to leave this magical spot, head initially in the direction of Angelokastro, down some flat rocks. You see a track below, and this is what you are making for. Bear to the right before you get to the end of the rocks and push your way down the steep, pathless hillside. The undergrowth is thick, and it is like walking through snow. The land flattens out in some disused terraces, and you make your best way down the terrace walls to reach the track you saw from above.

Here turn left and follow the track across lovely heathland to regain the main walk near the shrine (near 10). Return to page 61 to complete the walk.

In Corfu's olive groves, the olive trees are individuals, and each sinuous trunk diffuses into a riot of angled branches topped by grey-green foliage. Usually they produce their fruit alternate years, and the crop is gathered when it falls into nets laid under the trees.

Four hundred years ago oil production of olive oil was negligible, and viniculture was the predominant concern. Then the Venetians, who ruled the island at that time, passed an ordinance enforcing the uprooting of the vines and the planting of olive trees in their place. More subtly, they offered an incentive in the form of a hundred gold pieces for every ten trees planted. As a result, the olive trees which blanket Corfu, more than three and a half million of them, were planted.

The pressing of the olive oil is automated now, and few of the old manual presses are left. However, you may see some of the old machinery abandoned close to villages, or used as decoration in a garden. The olive pressing process was thus: A circular stone platform constituted the crushing bed of the press, where the raw olives were pulped. A great beam supported the upright granite millstones, which were turned by a lesser beam harnessed to a donkey. Adjacent was the press itself, a wooden frame holding a great screw, turned by a branch-sized lever. Under it, the olive pulp was placed in spherical baskets or rough sacks, from which, under pressure, the viscid oil would ooze, and, aided by a dash of hot water, would gush down gutters, bound for underground settling tanks.

There the oil, lighter than water, would rise and be scooped out into receptacles for storage.

WALK 15   Krini and Angelokastro

ANCIENT WAY to a MEDIEVAL FORTRESS

There are two ways to reach the medieval fortress of Angelokastro, near Paleokastritsa. Either you can follow the signs from the village of Krini, along the asphalt road which provides direct access for tourists and other visitors, to the foot of the pinnacle on which the ruins stand. Or you can sneak up on it from behind, using the little-known footpaths which connect the village with its ancient and beautiful olive groves. Thus, a simple trip to a spectacular sight becomes a lovely walk through unexplored countryside.

START at the Makrades/Krini/Vistonas crossroads.

GETTING THERE

By bus: Makrades; 06.15, 14.00 from Avramiou Street Bus Station (green bus). Or get the Paleokastritsa bus and combine the walk with Walk 14 (A).

By car: Take the Paleokastritsa road, and jsut before the resort, take the road signposted Lakones. Proceed through Lakones, past Bella Vista, and the next village is your starting point.

DURATION 2 hours.

ASCENT 300 metres in three sections. Very steep to Angelokastro.

TERRAIN Stony footpaths, some rough, and tracks.

SHADE Shady through olive groves. No shade elsewhere.

VIEWS Spectacular views from Angelokastro.

SIGHTS Medieval fortress.

AMENITIES Traditional coffee bar and Sunset Restaurant at Krini.

PICNIC On the threshing floor at Krini, or in Angelokastro, perhaps in the shade the oak tree just inside the curtain wall.

EQUIPMENT Strong walking boots. Trousers recommended.

Start at 1 by taking the road towards Makrades village, past the school. Take the first road (unmade) left then, a few minutes down, turn sharp left along a cobbled path (2). The path leads across a cultivated plain and then ascends to Krini. At a crossing alley, turn left to continue the walk, or go right to a threshing floor (3), reached by following the alley to where it leaves the village, then going left where the path forks. The view from this ancient structure is stunning. Returning to the main walk, the alley takes you into the little diamond-shaped village square.

Map - WALK 15

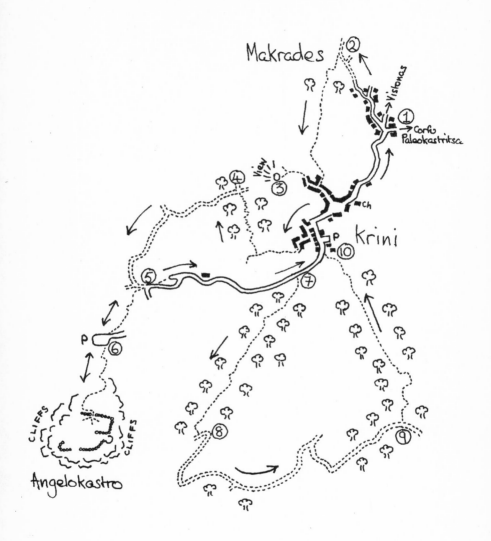

Take the road to the right and proceed to a 90° left-hand bend. Immediately after the turn, take a wide alley between two buildings, then go left and follow the main alley. Then keep left, squeeze beteen two cottages and leave the village along a narrow footpath. Go right at a junction, whereafter the way continues as a walled path descending through olive groves in sharp zig-zags.

When it meets an earth track at 4, go left. Your first view of Angelokastro comes soon, sudden and quite spectacular. The track meets an asphalt road on the elbow of a bend (5). Just before the asphalt, look on the right for a path (obscure), which leads you down steeply to the parking area at the foot of the climb to the ruins (6).

The ascending path is ahead, and after a sharp climb, you reach a rocky area under the corner of the fortifications. Here the path deviates right and then doubles back alongside the walls, runs under an arch and enters the castle through a tunnelled gateway. Paths radiate to various sights within the walls.

Caution - no safety barriers protect the sheer drop to the sea from the walls. Take care of children and dogs and do not approach the edge.

After your exploration of the fortress, return to 6 and ascend (you can take the road instead of the path). Return to Krini and your starting point, or extend the walk by leaving the road at 7, where you see a clear footpath on the right, descending steeply between rough walls. This ancient way, sometimes walled, sometimes leading through fissures in the rocks, and sometimes overgrown, used to lead all the way to the sea, but its lower reaches are now closed. Its surface is at times in bad condition.

The Fortress of Angelocastro was probably built during the 12th century as part of a great ring of forts which protected the island. From its summit, on a clear day, you can see the headland beyond the Gouvia Marina, where the defensive tower of the Kontokalis family mansion served as a beacon point to warn Angelokastro of the approach of Turkish raiders and pirates.

Thanks to its precipitous location, the fortress was never taken by force, and on more than one occasion it saved the local people from death at the hands of invaders, most notably during Turkish sieges during the 16th century, when up to 4000 villagers escaped death by taking refuge within its walls.

The event is difficult to imagine now, for little of the former defences still stand, and only their remains are scattered around the summit. The Church of the Archangels Michael and Gabriel, from which the fort takes its name, is intact, and seven graves hewn from solid rock lie close by. Near the main postern gate is a cave with the tiny chapel of Agia Kyriaki built into its wall. The cave was once used as a hermitage.

High on the campanile of the church in Krini village you can make out delightful, naïve carvings of the two Archangels. Lower down is a plaque carved with the symbol of Byzantium, the double-headed eagle.

After Angelokastro comes into sight high up to the right, you reach a point where the way ahead is completely choked. Here, your route continues up a steep bank to the left and emerges onto a gravel track on a sharp bend (8). Take the uphill way and proceed to a track which leads off on the right, at 8 (it comes AFTER a red-roofed building is sighted in the distance ahead). Take this track, which enters some olive groves and starts to descend, curving to the right.

As the descent begins, start looking for a path on the left (at 9. Its start, over a rock, is obscure; if you get to the bottom of the hill you have missed it and must return and look again). The path runs along the top of a bank, then alongside a wall, and reaches the Angelokastro road on the edge of Krini (10). Turn right and return to your starting point at the Makrades crossroads by following the main village road.

WALK 16   Roda to Episkepsis

ANCIENT OLIVE GROVES, VERDANT VALLEY

Leaving a busy resort, you are quickly in a land which time forgot. Ruins are dispersed in a forest of ancient olive trees as the way wanders along a ridge. Then you visit a village where tradition is a way of life, and return through a lush valley.

START At the crossroads at Roda.

GETTING THERE

By bus: Roda: 4-5 buses a day from Avramiou Street Bus Station (green bus).

By car: Take either the main north-east coast road, passing Kassiopi and Acharavi. Or take the Paleokastritsa road, turning left for Skripero and Roda; follow the signs. Park on the inland (Sfakera) side of the crossroads, to avoid crossing the busy road.

DURATION 4 to 5 hours.

ASCENT 300 metres.

TERRAIN Mostly tracks.

SHADE Mixed.

AMENITIES Coffee bars in Episkepsis.

PICNIC In the olive groves on the ascent, or in the fields at the valley side on the descent (not in cultivation).

EQUIPMENT Walking boots recommended.

Leave the crossroads (1) by the road towards Sfakera, then immediately take the first road on the right, signposted Kavalouri and Agraphi (Caution - this road is busy). Proceed past villas to an extensive plastic greenhouse beside the road on the left (2), at which point you take a track to the left.

You then take the first track on the left, which near Sfakera meets a road, where you go right. A short distance on, look on the left for a concrete ramp (3), which takes you into the village. Go straight on through the houses, and you meet a road close to a sharp corner. Here go left and then right at the next road, a concrete alley leading up between houses (Note the fine building on the right).

Leading out of the houses, the road becomes a track ascending through pretty countryside, and views of the sea begin to open behind you.

Map - WALK 16

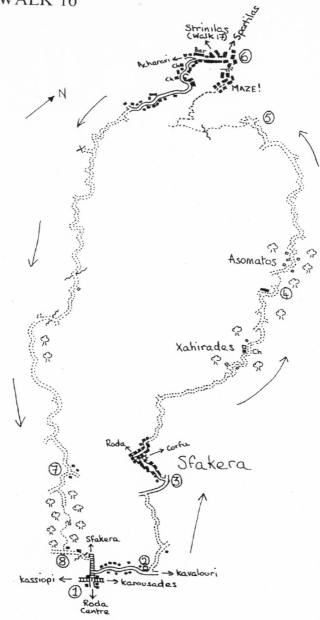

Into olive groves, the track starts to pass some ruined cottages, and the very old, now restored, church of Saint George. Ignore all joining tracks. Continue to a large house fronted with a flower-filled garden, after which you take a footpath (the old way) to join the track again a little further up. You are now on a ridge, where there are more ruins amongst the trees, and soon you see Episkepsis ahead.

Eventually, you reach a crossroads (5), where you take the footpath which goes sharply left. The old cobbled way into the village, the path descends to cross a stream. A few steps after the bridge, fork right and climb the rough path to the village, entering it through a maze of alleyways. A flight of shallow steps leads up to the main village road at 6, and a left turn brings you to the village centre where there are some bars.

Here you may begin your return to Roda, or you may continue to Strinilas (Walk 17).

To return to Roda, leave the main village road by way of a road on the left. It passes two churches and some houses, then becomes a track, descending quite sharply. Ignore a track to the right which snakes downhill. The way takes you down into a verdant valley and along it, crossing the river twice. Note the atrractive views all around and especially behind you.

Keep to the main track, and eventually you meet a wide gravel road beside some houses (7). Here go right, then take the next track to the left, a grassy way which leads into an extensive grove of olive trees planted in straight lines on the flat land. Soon the track fades out, and you continue along an indistinct path. Reaching a hut, you bear slightly right, then follow your nose towards a white villa visible through the line of trees.

Beside the villa, you reach at 8 a gravel road. Here go left, and you soon join the main Sfakera road again, with the crossroads a short walk to your right.

Map - WALK 17

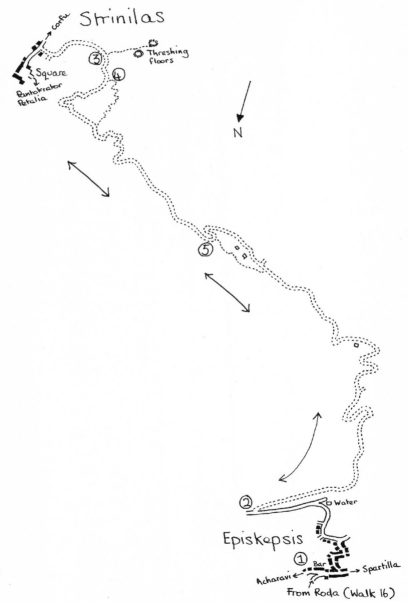

Strinilas

Corfu

③

Threshing floors

Square

Pantokrator Petalia

④

N

⑤

② Water

Episkepsis

① Bar

Acharavi ← → Spartilla

From Roda (Walk 16)

WALK 17   Episkepsis to Strinilas

APPROACH TO THE MOUNTAIN

Episkepsis is a village between plain and mountain; Strinilas belongs purely to the mountain. During this walk, you make the transition from one sphere to another, from a village which overlooks verdant olive groves, to one high on the bare mountain.

START In Episkepsis, at the bars by the road (end of Walk 16).

GETTING THERE

By bus: Agios Panteleimonas: 05.00, 14.00 from Avramiou Street Bus Station (green bus).

By car: Take the main coast road north through Ipsos, then turn up to Spartilas, after which you continue downhill 7 kilometres to Episkepsis.

On foot: From Roda (Walk 16).

DURATION 2 to 3 hours, there and back. From Roda to Strinilas and back, allow 6 to 8 hours. If you wish to continue to Pantokrator along marked roads (not illustrated), allow an additional 3 to 4 hours. Unless you are super-fit and walk fast, or start at dawn, you will not be able to reach the Pantokrator summitstarting from Roda, and return the same day. You could, however, get a friend in a car to meet you at, say, Strinilas as you return.

ASCENT 350 metres (700 metres altogether to the summit from Episkepsis).

TERRAIN Mostly stony track.

SHADE None.

VIEWS Spectacular scenery.

SIGHTS Two threshing floors, one mountain village.

AMENITIES Several restaurants in Strinilas.

PICNIC On one of the threshing floors.

EQUIPMENT Strong walking boots. If you are continuing to Pantokrator, take extra clothing, wet weather gear, and full supplies and equipment as specified in the introduction.

Starting at the bars (at 1, which is the end of Walk 16), head along the village road in the direction of Spartilas. Just a few metres on, take an alley leading sharp left, where you ascend a flight of wide steps. At the top, turn right, then left, and you will reach a road. Here go left, and proceed past the water building, after which you take a rough gravel road sharp right (2). You now begin a long ascent which takes you to Strinilas.

Reaching Strinilas, fork right, then go left at the road with Chronis Restaurant opposite, to reach the village square with its majestic elm tree which shades two or three more restaurants.

You may continue to the Pantokrator summit from here (not illustrated; the way is signposted), but remember that it will take you several hours to reach the summit and return.

Return the same way to Episkepsis.

THREE DETOURS ON YOUR RETURN TRIP ARE OPTIONAL:

At 3, a short distance below Strinilas, a path on the left leads down to two threshing floors (this path does not continue further).

At 4, a little further down, a section of the old path descends steeply to the track again. This path is rather overgrown at its lower end.

At 5, leave the track on the outside of the sharp left-hand bend to pick up the old path, which descends to flat terraces and gradually converges with the track again.

You can, of course, walk the route in reverse, starting at Strinilas.

WALK 18   Agia Ekaterini Headland

UNSPOILT COAST AND A RUINED MONASTERY

A coastline without any development is a rarity on an island which lives from tourism. And here, at the far northern tip of Corfu, is such a coast; a coast where the sea batters the rocky shoreline and washes into sandy coves, and only the elements belong.

START At Agios Spiridon Bay.

GETTING THERE

> By bus: Loutses - Kassiopi: Every two hours from Avramiou Street Bus Station (green bus). Get off at Perithia and walk about 1 kilometre to Agios Spiridon.
>
> By car: Main coast road north-east from Town. Five kilometres after Kassiopi, turn right for Agios Spiridon (signposted). Park by beach.

DURATION 2 to 3 hours, depending how far you go.

ASCENT Negligible.

TERRAIN Earth tracks and footpaths, some with sharp stones.

SHADE None except around monastery.

SIGHTS Abandoned monastery. Northernmost point of Corfu.

SWIMMING Several excellent spots on sandy beaches. Agios Spiridon Bay and Almiros are among the best beaches on the island.

AMENITIES Tavernas at Agios Spiridon and Almiros (summer only).

PICNIC Anywhere along the coast.

EQUIPMENT Strong closed shoes essential for the footpaths. Swimming gear.

Start behind the beach at Agios Spiridon Bay (1), and take the road between the beach and Lake Antiniotissa. Shortly, you cross a bridge and enter the exposed Agia Ekaterini headland, where the way is a gravel track.

At a crossing of tracks (2), take the track to the right, which stops at a beach. Turn left along the beach, then leave it just as the sand finishes. Here you pick up a narrow path which runs parallel with the coast. The path, blazed in the red soil by sheeps' pattering feet, is visible across knife-sharp rocks and through low bushes. You pass the beacon (3) marking the most northerly point of Corfu, after which the path passes behind a beach, where it becomes a track. This track then meets a more defined track (4), where you turn right.

(If you wish to cut the walk short at this point, turn left instead of right and pass through the monastery grounds to 8, and return thereafter to your starting point.)

Map - WALK 18

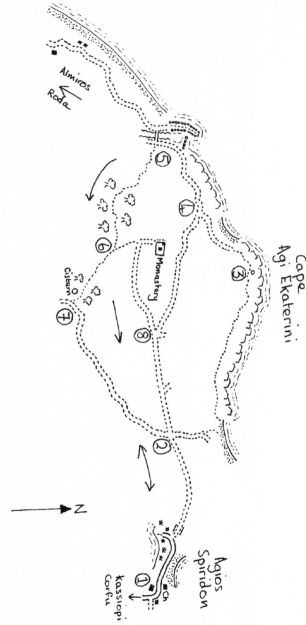

Almiros
Roda

Cape
Agi Ekaterini

Monastery

Cistern

Agios
Spiridon

Kassiopi
Corfu

Ch

Z

Having turned right at 4, you follow the track to the point where it stops at a footbridge (5). The way across the footbridge leads to the wide, sandy beach of Almiros and eventually to Acharavi and Roda.

Continue the walk by taking a narrow goat path which begins exactly opposite the footbridge and runs up the hillside. At the top of the rise, the path runs through unkempt olive groves. It hits a crossing path at 6.

To reach the monastery, go left here and almost immediately you meet a drive which, to the left, runs to the (locked) gate. Alongside the wall beside the gate, a path leads to steps up to a tower which overlooks the monastery grounds. From the main gate, you may follow the access drive to return directly to your starting point, passing point 8.

Alternatively, return to 6 and continue along the path through a tunnel of bushes and then into an olive grove. Here the path is less clear; you go straight on, pass a water cistern on your right and hit a track (7).

Here turn left and follow the track back to the first crossroads at 2 and thereafter back to your starting point at Agios Spiridon.

Map - WALK 19

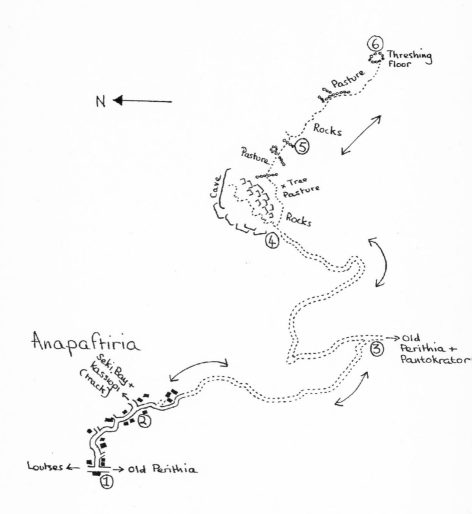

WALK 19   Anapaftiria and the Cave

A CAVE AND A THRESHING FLOOR

It's a truly dramatic sight. You climb above Loutses into a high region of limestone rocks, which appear to go on forever. Then without warning a chasm opens at your feet, and you descend into the cool shade of the cave mouth.

START Just beyond Loutses, at the Anapaftiria road junction.

GETTING THERE

> By bus: Loutses - Kassiopi: Every two hours from Avramiou Street Bus Station (green bus).

> By car: Main coastal road past Kassiopi. 5 kilometres after Kassiopi, turn left for Loutses. Park beside the road after the Anapaftiria junction, but not in the wide section where the bus turns round.

DURATION 1 ^{1}/2 hours to the cave and back. 2 hours to the threshing floor (6) and back.

ASCENT 200 metres in a steady climb from 2 to 4.

TERRAIN Graded track to the cave (4). Very rocky terrain, some parts without a clear path, between 4 and 6.

SHADE None.

VIEWS Coastal view from 6. Views over Loutses and to coast while decending.

SIGHTS A cave and a threshing floor!

AMENITIES None on the route. Traditional bars in Loutses.

PICNIC On the threshing floor.

EQUIPMENT Ordinary closed shoes as far as 4. Boots and trousers needed between 4 and 6.

Start at 1 by taking the road signposted Anapaftiria, and after passing some houses, take a concrete road to the right (2). After another little settlement, the road becomes a gravel track, climbing steadily. At a junction of tracks (3) turn sharp left, and then continue to climb to the cave, with short level stretch before you reach the edge of the huge chasm, where the track stops (4). You descend to the bottom of the chasm by way of a steep footpath, which takes you under the overhanging cliff and into the cave itself, used by shepherds as a sheep shelter. Return to 4.

Now you may return to your starting point, following the guide below, or continue to the threshing floor. Because paths are not always clear, make sure you look back frequently on this section to see your return route.

Facing the chasm at the top of the footpath, go to the right, where you should be able to make out a sheep path up the rocky slope. Soon you reach a small plateau, where the path fades out altogther. Here bear left, heading for a thorn tree. Passing to the left of this tree, you pick up the path again, leading over a rocky col and down into a pasture in a hollow. Reaching the pasture, head for a ruined stone shelter on the other side, then turn right and make for the edge of the hollow. Passing through the gap in a broken wall (5), bear right and follow a narrow path through standing rocks. Soon a valley with two narrow terrace walls comes into sight. The animals have made a path up the terraces, which you follow to the top terrace, where your destination comes into sight ahead at the far side - the curved wall of the threshing floor (6). The stone slabs of its base are intact, and there is a very fine view over Cape Varvaras and Avlaki Bay.

Return to 4, and then down the track back to your starting point.

The circular threshing floors (*aloni*) with their flat paving stones were always sited in places exposed to the wind to facilitate the winnowing of grain. There are many in mountain regions and also some beside the sea. The one above the cave is especially well preserved.

WALK 20   Kassiopi - Bodolakos

A WILDERNESS near a BUSY RESORT

The hinterland of Kassiopi is harsh. From the fertile coast, the mountainslopes rise above the azure sea to form a landscape of knife-sharp rocks, of spiky vegetation, of deserted hamlets and deep, shady gorges; the timeless, awe-inspiring scenery of Greece, all stillness and solitude.

START At Imerolia just north of Kassiopi, or in Kassiopi village square.

GETTING THERE

By bus: Loutses - Kassiopi: Every two hours from Avramiou Street Bus Station (green bus).

By car: Follow the main north-east coast road to Imerolia, just past Kassiopi. Park at the side of the road. Or start and finish the walk at Kassiopi.

DURATION 2 to 3 hours.

ASCENT 300 metres in two steep stages.

TERRAIN Rough footpaths with loose stones. Some pathless walking through prickly vegetation.

SHADE Almost none.

VIEWS Excellent views of Kassiopi and the coast.

SIGHTS Deserted villages, derelict windmill.

AMENITIES None, except in Imerolia and Kassiopi (summer).

PICNIC At the derelict windmill in Kelia.

EQUIPMENT Strong walking boots and trousers essential.

If you start at Kassiopi, take the road towards Roda. The road joins the main road then sweeps around the coastline of Imerolia Bay, and on the hillside ahead you can see the path you will be taking. Proceed along the main road as far as the little harbour of Imerolia (1). Alternatively, start at Imerolia.

More or less opposite the harbour, the path leaves the road, running first towards a house and then climbing in zig-zags behind the regional High School, with an opening vista of Kassiopi and the coastline behind. Where a track from the right joins the path (2) keep going straight on to pick up the old path again.

Then Kassiopi disappears from view and the way becomes less steep, as the path ascends a once-cultivated valley. Deserted buildings (Lower Bodolakos) are in sight ahead, and you aim for these when the path becomes indistinct.

Map - WALK 20

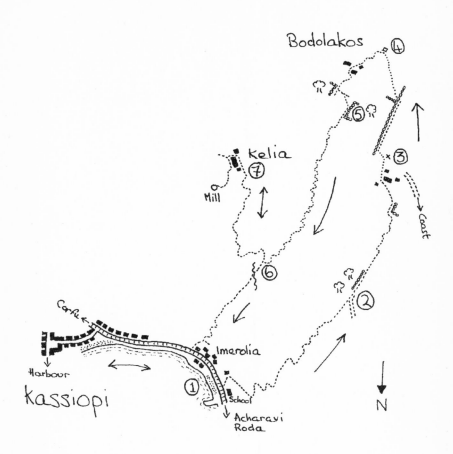

Bodolakos

④

⑤

Kelia

⑦

Mill

③

Coast

⑥

②

Corfu

Imerolia

Harbour

Kassiopi

①

School

Acharavi
Roda

N

When you reach the houses, head left along the front and around the corner, whereafter you aim for a solitary olive tree. At the tree, go diagonally left to a drystone wall, then continue alongside it. You can see your objective ahead and to the left - another huddle of abandoned houses.

(A track has recently been bulldozed to Lower Bodolakos, and at the time of writing plans were underway to drive it on through to the higher settlement. Once it is in place, just ignore the next paragraph and take the track, picking up the directions again when you reach the front of the hamlet.)

There being no clear path in this section of the walk, to reach the houses you follow the wall to its junction with another wall which cuts down the gully on the left. Here scramble over the wall you have followed into the far field, then make your way down the gully and up the other side, aiming for a tin hut which is visible on the skyline. At the hut (4), you pick up a path leading down to the houses.

Proceed to the front of the hamlet, where another clear path begins and runs towards a walled olive grove on the right. Take the first path left at a fork and then the next path right, which goes directly to the neat wall of another olive grove (5) and then alongside it. At the lower corner of the enclosure, the path steepens into a gully, which it descends on a cobbled surface in series of tight switchbacks.

At the foot of the gully as it meets another valley, the path divides (6), and here you may take a detour: Take the right hand way, which climbs the opposite valley-side steeply. After a rough gate, you breast the hill and approach the back of the hamlet of Kelia (7). Go through another gate, then around to the front of the buildings, where you turn left and follow a walled path through more gates to a disused windmill, which you could see from the path below. Return to 6.

Take the downhill path at 6, which leads you across a stream bed and along a valley to reach the main road at Imerolia.

WILD FLOWERS OF CORFU

Corfu is famous as being the greenest of all the Greek island. Its typical Mediterranean climate - mild wet winter and hot, dry summers - mean that wild and cultivated plants grow in profusion. There are forty-three varieties of orchid alone *, in addition to many of the common European wild flowers which the visitor can easily recognise. For the identification of rarer species, and those indigenous to Greece, a wild flower book will be required.

Spring is the best time for wild flowers, but the season does not reach all localities at the same time. Seashore plants which were dormant throughout the summer drought sprout in the winter rains and by February coastlines are a blaze of colour. As the sun warms the soil, the flowers of the lowland zone (sea level to 700 metres, which comprises most of Corfu) come into bloom. April and May are the months during which most flowers blossom, and as the days lengthen towards midsummer, the sequence of flowering advances to higher altitudes. In Corfu, only the Pantokrator Massif is classed as 'mountain zone' and here as late as June are to be found numerous upland species as well as many plants which flowered earlier at lower altitudes. Here, the rocky hillsides are like a garden in May, with a profusion of orchids as well as many other flowers.

July and August are the hottest and driest months and the least rewarding for botanists, although there are several species which defy the drought and come to the peak of their flowering. In September and October, after the late summer thunderstorms, a 'second spring' begins with the appearance of cyclamen and crocus which carpet woodland banks as the spring flowers carpeted the olive groves.

Winter is generally mild and the growing season hardly ceases. With February, warmer days come, hastening the passage to a colourful spring.

* One of the best orchid paths is the section of Walk 23 between points 11 and 12. We have counted up to 14 different species on this path, including Giant, Yellow Bee, Bumble Bee, Brown Bee, Woodcock, Tongue, Man, Naked Man, Four-spotted, Loose-flowered and Monkey. The best time is April and early May, when many species grow simultaneously.

WALK 21   Nissaki to Pantokrator Summit

ASCENT of CORFU'S HIGHEST MOUNTAIN

The most arduous, but most spectacular and rewarding walk on the island. The breathtaking grandeur of the scenery, the incredible variety of flora and the final exhilaration of making it to the peak will conspire to make this day on the mountain the most memorable of your stay on Corfu.

START At Nissaki, opposite the entrance to the Magic Life Hotel (formerly Club Med.).

GETTING THERE

By bus: Loutses - Kassiopi: Every two hours approx from Avramiou Street Bus Station (green bus).

By car: Take the main north-east coast road as far as the starting point. Park beside the road just before the start.

DURATION Walk A: Allow 8 to 9 hours for the complete walk. Walk B: 3 to 4 hours.

ASCENT: Walk A: 914 metres, plus small ascents on return route. Walk B: 400 metres.

TERRAIN Rough tracks and some very tough footpaths.

SHADE None except at start and finish.

VIEWS Spectacular from all parts of the walk.

SIGHTS The Pantokrator summit and monastery. Deserted villages.

AMENITIES None at all on the route.

PICNIC Walk A: Snack on the ascent, and if you want a full picnic, leave it to Old Sinies on your way down. Walk B: The Shepherd's Plateau - you can look at Pantokrator, where you're not going.

EQUIPMENT Strong, comfortable walking boots, waterproofs, extra clothing, safety equipment, water and food, and full supplies as specified in the introduction.

WALKS A & B: Start both walks by taking the rough steps directly opposite the entrance to the hotel, next to a bar (1). The stepped path ascends steeply. Amongst some chicken runs just above the road, the path goes right, and then goes right again about 50 metres after passing close to the left of a house (yellow markers guide you). Thereafter the path continues to climb some distance through olive groves terraced with curved drystone walls, and the way is mostly cobbled.

At 2 the path then meets a concrete road just below Katavolos. Here you go right, uphill. Look on the right for break in the wall where a path leads you into a paved area, formerly the 'village square', shaded by a giant ilex tree.

Map - WALK 21

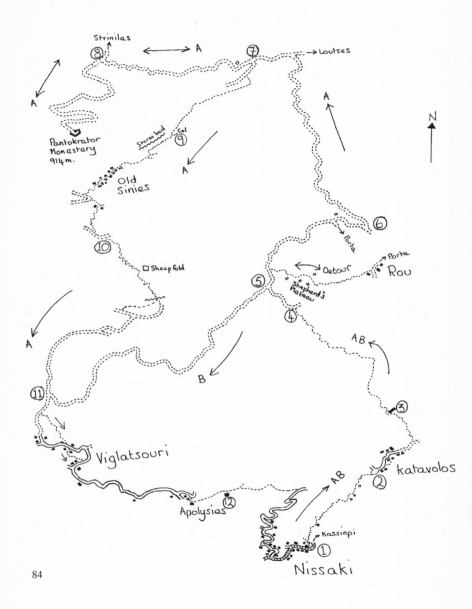

Leave this little square along an alleyway, which takes you back onto the road. Turn right and ascend past another group of houses, after which the road becomes a track. A hundred metres or so further on, look on the left for a narrow path, which leads you steeply uphill to reach a row of deserted houses (3). The path skirts round the left of the building, and the yard at the rear is a shady spot to recover your breath.

The path, less steep now, continues behind the houses, and soon leaves the belt of forest above the olive groves to emerge onto the open hillside. Sweeping around the curve of the hill, it then climbs sharply to meet a track at 4, where you go left. Soon the track meets another one at 5, and here the routes of Walks A and B diverge. However, if you are following Walk B, a detour to the Shepherd's Plateau and Rou is recommended. Directions for Walk B are on page 87.

DETOUR TO ROU: At 5 turn right. A water pipe runs alongside the road on the right. The pipe is cemented down in places, and you must look for a section of pipe which runs under a long ridge of cement - about 70 metres from 5. Here you turn off the track and follow a trail beaten out by sheep to the top of the ridge. A splendid view opens out, and you descend an indistinct path to the plateau below, where tall ilex trees provide shade. A threshing floor, several stone bothies and two water cisterns are nearby. The path to Rou continues from the ilex trees, runs alongside a drystone wall and across a pasture, then, much eroded, plunges downhill. Soon you reach Rou, deserted except for an English couple. Return to 5.

WALK A: For the Pantokrator summit, turn right at 5 and proceed to the first junction of tracks, where you take the left fork. At the next junction (6), you go sharp left. The track now makes a steady ascent, with the rocky hillside falling away to the left. Eventually, the track which ascends from Loutses joins from the right, and you head straight on for the next junction (7).

(This junction is sited on a col where the old paths over and across the massif used to meet. To the north, you can just see the houses of Perithia below.)

Having reached 7, you may continue to the Pantokrator summit (note that you will need at least another two hours to get to the summit and back) or you may abandon the ascent and begin your return. If you choose the latter, skip the next paragraph.

To continue to Pantokrator, take the right hand fork at 7. This track climbs to meet the main Pantokrator road at 8, just below the final ascent to the summit. Thereafter it is a rather boring climb, but worth it for the achievement, if not for the sight of a plethora of telecommunications masts. Return to the col (7).

Now take the downhill track, but before you begin to descend, look on the hillside just below the scar made by bulldozing the new track. You should be able to make out the line of the old footpath, which runs parallel with the track and just below it. You must descend to this path, and you gain it by scrambling, with great care, down the scree on the left of the track, a hundred metres or so along it (marked with yellow arrows). At the foot of the scree, follow yellow markers to pick up the path, which you follow around the side of the basin and then to a small col (9).

After crossing the col, the path makes a steep descent along the left side of a deep V-shaped gully, parallel with the dry floodwater bed. The path is not always clear, and you have to pick your best way over loose stones and shale. The houses of Old Sinies come into sight ahead. Then, towards the bottom of the gully, you bear left over the small rise to reach a pasture where a clear earth path runs downhill and then heads straight for Old Sinies.

Passing a stone well-head, the path leads into the village, with its ruined, roofless houses (beware if you intend to explore; the ruins are unstable). Look on the left for a church with frescoes, and do not fail to look behind you to see the former extent of this abandoned settlement.

Continue to follow the path until, after the last houses, you drop to a track. Turn left here and walk a few metres to the hairpin bend, where you leave the track on its elbow, following the gravel of the dry stream bed for a few metres and then scrambling up a bank towards two more ruins, where you meet a clear path (the way from now on is marked with blue spots). Go right, and top a small rise (a fine threshing floor is on the right), where the path, rather indistinct, drops to the track again.

Here turn left, and around a gentle bend start looking on the right for a path (10 - marked with yellow markers and blue spots) where you leave the track again. Your way is now a clear path, cobbled in places, which descends the steep hillside in a series of short switchbacks, passes a large sheep enclosure and reaches the valley bottom.

After crossing the stream bed, the path climbs to meet a track. Go left and right at the next track (this is the same track that you quit below Old Sinies; but in order to avoid gradients it has made a detour of several kilometres). Now you make a gentle descent towards Viglatsouri, passing a junction of tracks at 11. Walk B rejoins the longer route here.

As the way, now on concrete, steepens, look on the left for a path (marked with red and yellow arrows), a quicker and pleasanter descent which rejoins the road lower down. (Don't worry if you miss it; just turn left at the next junction.)

A few steps down the road, take another cut-off beside a house, and again rejoin the road further down. After this cut-off, take the first road left, which descends and then briefly climbs to Apolysies. Take the first road left into the settlement and on the first bend, next to a house on the right, go down some steps and then bear left along a footpath. The way runs more or less level and passes to the rear of a large villa (12). When the path forks soon after the villa, make sure you take the right-hand way. Follow the path to join a road, and turn right downhill. A walk of 15 minutes or so will take you down to the main road at Nissaki, and your starting point is close by to the left.

WALK B: You have taken the downhill way at 5. Now you follow the track, with almost aerial views over Nissaki and to Corfu Town, and later towards Barbati. Eventually, the track meets the descending way from Old Sinies at 11. Here you turn left and should now complete the walk by following the main guide, starting on the previous page.

MONUMENT OF A PAST AGE

Old Perithia sits in a hollow in the mountain massif, its stone-built houses and terraced gardens surrounded by bare hillsides. But no eyes look out from empty windows, the cobbled streets are silent, and the formerly fruitful soil is choked with weeds. For the village, like many of the isolated and abandoned hamlets which are a feature of the Pantokrator Massif, is virtually deserted.

Its story is typical of the villages and hamlets which you pass on walks through this mountainous region. Old Perithia was established during Byzantine times when pirate raids forced people to abandon fertile coastal plains and hide themselves in inaccessible regions. Its location is perfect. Shut off from pirate's eye view by a conical mound, it is nevertheless accessible from the coast by a succession of connecting valleys. Driven into the mountains, villagers made the daily trip to their holdings on the coast, and returned in the evening. But there was another reason the mountain made better habitation, even after the danger of pirate raids ended with the final defeat of the Turks; the coastal lake, Antiniotissa (Walk 18), was infested with malaria-carrying mosquitoes, while the hill air was pure. Then in this century two factors combined to reverse the migration. With the use of insecticides mosquitoes diminished and the coast became a healthier place. Many of the villagers moved closer to the sea and others emigrated to American in search of a better life. Then tourism came, and the very inaccessability that had sustained the village drove its population away from it, nearer to the 'crock of gold'.

The abandoned terraces which climb in staircases up every gully, providing pockets of flat land for cultivation, testify to the formerly thriving population which inhabited these mountain villages - Old Sinies, Koromila, Bodholakos, Kelia, Rou.

In Old Perithia, there are many dwellings to explore, terraces of cottages beside the main cobbled street and, along footpaths, farmsteads with staircase and balcony leading to living quarters over ground floor barn. Though the houses are built solidly, one sometimes wonders whether the roof will cave in or the floorboards crumble under your feet. In several houses there remains an odd scrap of furniture - a version of the Victorian corner cabinets, or a table, or a chair with the familiar hessian seat. Many houses have their original bread ovens. A stone arch, bearing a crest, leads into to the grounds of the Skordilis Mansion, the wealthiest house in the village.

There are innumerable churches but only one is open, complete with icons painted on the doors. Wealthy families would put their spare cash to the glory of God - a form of insurance payment! - and dedicate their own personal church.

Wild flowers abound and fig, jujube, quince, almond and walnut trees bear fruit according to the season. And seasons change, and the years pass by, but Old Perithia remains as a monument of a past age.

WALK 22   Petalia - Old Perithia - Koromila

WILD MOUNTAIN SCENERY

Bare hills of limestone karst and deserted villages await you on this walk, and perhaps you will not see a soul but for a solitary shepherd. But in past days a thriving population was resident in this region, and you will see the cultivation terraces where they grew their grains and vegetables, the substantial houses which they built; all abandoned now.

START At Petalia, where just after you enter the village, the street widens on both sides.

GETTING THERE

By bus: Lakfi: 05.00, 14.00 from Avramiou Street Bus Station (green bus).

By car: Take the main road north. Turn right at Tzavros to Dassia and Ipsos. After climbing out of Ipsos, turn right for Spartilas. About one kilometre after Spartilas, follow signs for Strinilas and Lafki. Petalia is the second village on this road. Park a little before the village, well in to the side of the road.

DURATION 3 hours for the short walk. Allow at least two hours extra to get to Old Perithia and back from 4, making around 5 to 6 hours for the entire walk (not including prolonged stop in Old Perithia).

ASCENT Sharp climb from 1 to 2. Thereafter mainly descent to 4, steep between 3 and 4. Several climbs and descents between 4 and 9, some steep. Descent from 4 to 5 and corresponding ascent on your return. Note that Petalia is 200 metres higher than Old Perithia, so your return is mainly ascent.

TERRAIN Mainly graded gravel tracks and rough footpaths. Some walking off footpaths.

SHADE None.

VIEWS Spectacular mountain scenery. Some excellent views to the coast.

SIGHTS Old Perithia, an abandoned village with many well-preserved stone-built houses.

AMENITIES Taverna in Old Perithia

PICNIC At Koromila, beside the shady well-head.

EQUIPMENT Boots and trousers essential.

Start as indicated in Petalia (1). Here take a railed concrete ramp which ascends on the right and after the last house becomes a cobbled footpath. Ascend the path up a narrow valley to meet a track beside a rain-water catchment reservoir (2). (On the immediate right this track joins the main road to the Pantokrator summit.) At 2 turn left and follow the track for about two miles, around hillsides with dramatic views to the coast, then through valleys with little patches of cultivation.

Map - WALK 22

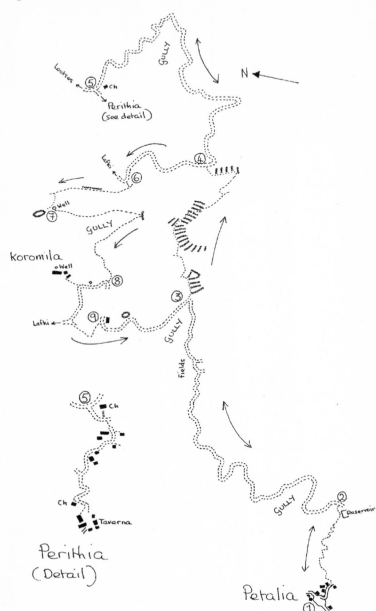

Lochros ←
⑤ ● Ch
Perithia
(see detail)

GULLY

N ←

Lafki
⑥
⑦ ● Well

GULLY

Koromila
● Well
⑧

Lafki ←
⑨

④

GULLY

③

Fields

⑤ Ch

Ch
Taverna

Perithia
(Detail)

GULLY

② ☐ Reservoir

Petalia ①

The track then crosses a level stretch, where white stones outline the meadows on the left, and enters a valley where you can see the track continuing on the opposite hillside. After descending, the track swings around the head of the gully in a sharp bend (3).

On the elbow of this bend, leave the track by an indistinct path into a descending valley. The valley floor is contoured with walled terraces and the path runs down the left bank of the 'staircase' of terraces, and you scramble down the low walls when necessary. After four or five of the terraces, you reach a triangular plot, which you immediately exit on the left, meeting a clear path just below, where you bear right.

The path crosses a valley head and a small stony ridge and then enters another valley where a staircase of terraces appears to flow down from the right. d Drop down into this valley and continue your descent down the terraces on their left bank. The houses of Perithia are in sight ahead. After crossing the head of a branching set of terraces, a clearer path crosses to the right side of the main terraces, whereupon the earth track you are making for comes into sight below. Either you can scramble down to the track directly, or you can follow the path as it veers away from the terraces, then go left at a junction of paths and continue to reach some more terraces, which you follow down to the earth track at 4. Here you may turn right to proceed to Perithia (see relevant section of this guide), or go left to Koromila.

TO KOROMILA: Turning left at 4, follow the track around a couple of bends, when you will see a clear path traversing the hillside ahead. You gain this path by leaving the track on the elbow of the next sharp right-hand bend (6), heading straight up towards a thorn tree. The narrow path ascends steadily, running partly on the low drystone wall which made it so conspicuous from below, until just under the top of the ridge, it fades out. Here head left, and after a few steps you cross the ridge; on the other side make for a stone enclosure and a well-head which you see just below.

Reaching these structures (7), turn left to follow a faint path which runs first alongside a fenced pocket of cultivation, then, becoming clearer, makes a decending traverse of the hill into the side valley. Two paths are visible climbing the opposite side of the gully, and you will take the lower one. The path you are following crosses the gully head beside a tall terrace wall, and then ascends to reach a track on a sharp bend at 8. Here take the right-hand way and descend to the houses of Koromila, which are reached via a short section of footpath. Behind a house which still wears traces of its original strawberry colour, there is a yard, and steps lead to a well-head shaded by trees - a fine spot for rest and refreshments.

Return to the first track and go right, past the orchard which gives the hamlet its name (crab apple). Then take the first track on the left, barely more than a path, which ascends steeply to meet the track again opposite an extensive sheep shelter constructed entirely of tin sheets (9). Here turn right and a walk of a few minutes will return you to 3, where you continue to follow the track to the rainwater reservoir at 2, whereafter you take the path to return to your starting point at Petalia.

TO PERITHIA: Having descended the terraces to the earth track at 4, turn right and simply follow the track to reach Perithia. The village seems close (and indeed is close as the crow flies) but the track, making a gradual descent for the benefit of vehicles, takes a convoluted route around gullies, and it will take you from 45 minutes to an hour to arrive at your destination.

The first building you reach is a church, after which you take the first track left, at 5. Just after you pass the church steps on the left, you take a path to the right which then widens and leads directly to the village square (This was the old village high street, and it is still entirely surfaced with cobbles). Refreshments await in the village square.

Return along the track to 4 and thereafter follow the guide as above to take you to Koromila and back to Petalia.

WALK 23   Spartilas - Zigos - Sokraki

HIGH MOUNTAIN VALLEYS

The periphery of the Pantokrator Massif has its own identity. On this walk, which covers part of a high plateau cut by deep river valleys, the scenery in places resembles Scotland, with evergreen trees on grey rocks, and in others is reminiscent of Tuscany.

START Anywhere in Spartilas, or at the village's western end at Asteras Bar.

GETTING THERE

By bus: Agios Panteleimonas: 05.00, 14.00 from Avramiou Street Bus Station (green bus).

By car: Follow main road north through Ipsos, then follow signs to Spartilas (steep road with many hairpin bends). Park at the far end of the village, well into the side, and not blocking any access. Or park at Asteras Bar at the very end of the village.

DURATION 4 to 6 hours. Allow at least an extra 2 to 3 hours to get to Troumpetta and back.

ASCENT The walk covers undulating ground on a high plateau; there are no severe climbs, though some gradients are prolonged.

TERRAIN Rough, stony paths with some scrambling involved. Also tracks and some road walking.

SHADE Shady along forest paths. Tracks and roads are in general without shade.

AMENITIES Coffee bars in Sokraki.

PICNIC In the yard behind the church, at 9.

EQUIPMENT Strong walking boots and trousers are essential.

Start at 1 by walking along the street away from the direction of Corfu Town (west). Just out of the village, take the second track on the left (2), which leads down onto an agricultural plateau planted mainly with vines.

Follow the track across the plateau until, after a short descent, it begins to climb. After ascending a short distance, you see a track going off left, whereafter you look on your right for a very indistinct track (3). A rock on the near corner is marked with a red spot, and similar spots now mark the way from time to time.

After a few metres, the indistinct track drops into an olive grove planted with young trees. Here there is no clear path, and you bear left, following the line of the terrace wall until you see a clear path again, which leads into cypress forest. In the forest, the path begins to climb a 'staircase' of walls which formed the now disused and overgrown terraces. Some walls require a scramble.

Map - WALK 23

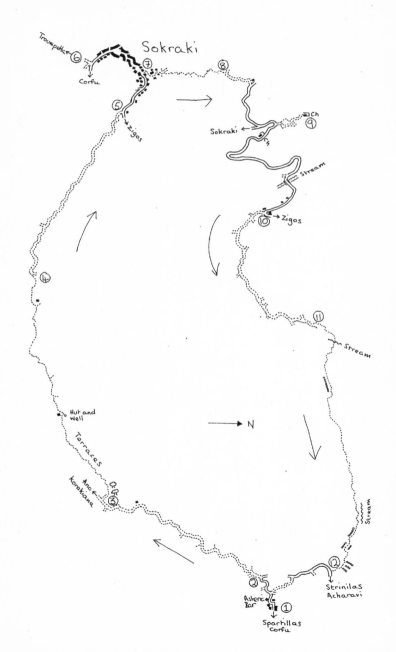

At the top of the staircase, the path reaches a hut and a well and immediately begins to descend disused but clearer terraces in the next valley. After a few terraces, the path starts to converge with the shrubs on the left of the valley, then it rejoins what must have been its old route along the margin of the cultivated land, running alongside drystone walls. In a clearing near a stone hut, fork left.

The next landmark comes when the path leads into an open space at 4, from where two tracks depart. Take the left hand one of the two, which ascends gently, first through shrubs and then beside extensive terraces, to cross a low pass into the descending valley, also with wide terraced fields.

The track now descends to meet a road on the edge of Sokraki (5). Proceed towards the village to the point where on the right you see a wide concrete path descending steeply beside a holding wall (7). Here the walk continues, but you may wish first to take refreshment in the tiny village square, which is reached after a short walk.

(Or you may proceed to Troumpetta: continue through the village until a view of Corfu Town opens on the left. The first track going right at 6 leads directly to Troumpetta. This section is not illustrated. If you have taken a bus to Spartilas and do not wish to return to your starting point, you may catch a bus to town from Troumpetta.)

Continuing the walk from 7, descend the concrete path to the point where, just after the houses stop, the track divides. Here go straight on, where, beside the wooden electricity post, you set off down a rough and stony path (a red spot marks the start of the path). At the foot of the sharp descent, where the path becomes a track (8), go straight on, then go right where the track meets road. At the next junction, where you reach the main Sokraki - Zigos road, go left. (On the elbow of the first sharp bend along this road, you may make a short ascent by a path or a track to reach an old but restored church at 9 where a walled grassy yard makes a perfect picnic spot.)

Now follow the road downhill, with a view of the houses of Zigos spreading along a low ridge. Descend to cross the river bridge, then, just as the road makes a last sharp left hand bend before reaching the houses of Zigos, take a track on the right (10).

A comparatively uninteresting section of the walk follows, as the track proceeds slowly up the narrowing valley amongst olive groves. Follow always the main track, straight ahead. Eventually, the track stops in an open space (11), which you cross and leave by a path on the left (red spots assist your way here again).

The path meanders amongst young cypress trees and then crosses a stream bed with, in winter, a waterfall and delightful rock pool. It then ascends quite sharply, and levels out on a disused and overgrown terrace. Here follow the line of the narrow terrace, which in some seasons is overgrown with bracken. At one point, the path ascends to a slightly higher level, but otherwise proceeds straight on. Red spots mark the route.

The Melisoudhi, whose stream you crossed, is at first far below, but eventually the path converges with the stream, which here, in winter, runs through a series of miniature waterfalls and rock pools, spoilt by litter washed down from higher up. The path, which is clearer now, then ascends between walls until it becomes blocked by shrubs. Here you continue to ascend the terraces beside the old path, and emerge suddenly onto a road at 12.

Turn right and proceed past a red villa and then past one which is painted ochre, with a garden of crazy paving. Just after, you see on the left a narrow track leading between low walls. This takes you back onto the road at the edge of Spartilas, beside the Asteras Bar.

MOUNTAINBIKE TOURS

WHERE TO RENT

THE CORFU MOUNTAINBIKE SHOP, Dassia. Tel. (0661) 93344, 97609, fax (0661) 36825. Quality mountainbikes for long or short term rent. Crash helmet, back-pack, first-aid kit and map supplied. Children's chair on request. Sponsored by Giant.

SOME SAFETY TIPS

KEEP always well in to the right of the road.

BEWARE of farmers trucks on minor roads.

GO EASY on the village wine - you've got to get home!

MOUNTAINBIKE TOUR 1

PYRGI - SPARTILAS - STRINILAS - PETALIA - LAFKI - PERITHIA
AGIOS SPIRIDON BEACH - ALMIROS BEACH - ACHARAVI
EPISKEPSIS - SGOURADES - ZIGOS - SOKRAKI
ANO KORAKIANA - AGIOS MARKOS - PYRGI (60 KILOMETRES)

THE PANTOKRATOR MASSIF

*Only for the fit and tough, this trip crosses the Pantokrator Massif twice.
The scenery is wild and the views are stupendous. You also pass through
unspoilt villages and visit two of the best sandy beaches on the island.*

START At Pyrgi

Start at **Pyrgi** by going north along the coast road, then take the road to
Spartilas, a very steep climb with many harpin bends. After Spartilas,
take the signposted road leading to **Strinilas** (a good spot for rest and
coffee in the famous village square) and **Lafki**. The descent begins after
Petalia.

*Note that if you take the Pantokrator road, just before Petalia, you gain
access to the network of gravel mountain roads as well as to the
Pantokrator summit (approximately 5 kilometres, the last one very steep).
This is excellent off-road cycling, but very rough and tough.*

After Lafki, take a road right which is signposted to Perithia. Go right at
the hamlet of **Vasilika**. Reaching **Perithia**, turn left, then left again at the
main road. Take the next turn right, signposted to Agios Spiridon.
Descend gently to **Agios Spiridon Beach**.

Continue along the road at the back of the beach. It crosses a bridge and,
entering the Agia Ekaterini headland, becomes dirt. Follow the track to a
footbridge, and cross the river to the **Almiros** side.

Continue along the track to **Acharavi**, where you take one of many access
roads to the main road. Now go to the roundabout in the village centre.
About 100 metres towards Roda, take a narrow road on the left,
signposted to Episkepsis.

You climb all the way, sometimes steeply, through **Episkepsis** and to
Sgourades. Just before Sgourades, take a road right to Zigos and Sokraki.
Descend to **Zigos**, go sharp left in the village, then climb again to
Sokraki. You've made it! It's downhill all the way from here.

After Sokraki, the road drops in very tight switchbacks and care is
required. At the bottom, you reach **Ano Korakiana**. Pass almost through
the village, then go straight on at a bend to Agios Markos. You can make
a fast descent from here through **Agios Markos** and back to **Pyrgi**.

MOUNTAINBIKE TOUR 2

GOUVIA - TEMBLONI - GIANNADES - ERMONES BEACH VATOS - GOUVIA (25 KILOMETRES)

CENTRAL COAST-TO-COAST
AND THE ROPA VALLEY

Cross the low range of hills in the centre of the island to the flat agricultural plain of Ropa. Pass through fertile valleys to a sandy beach, and return by back roads through fields and olive groves.

START At the Gouvia crossroads by Fillipas Restaurant

Starting at the crossroads at **Gouvia**, take the road signposted Tembloni and Danilia. Turn right after the level stretch and at the top of the climb, turn sharp right. Proceed, mainly climbing, to **Tembloni**. After Tembloni, the road descends steeply (views over Ropa Valley and to Giannades) to the main road.

Turn right at the main road, then after 400 metres take a minor road left. Cross the **Ropa Plain**, then head up towards Giannades. At a crossroads, you may continue on to **Giannades** village, or turn left on the road signposted Ermones. This narrow road leads along a verdant little valley, and meets the Ermones road. Turn right for **Ermones Beach**, where the road stops.

Return from Ermones along the road, and cross the river by way of the old stone bridge. Climb steeply to **Vatos**. After Vatos the road is downhill. Take the first asphalt road to the right, then the first to the left. Descend on this narrow road to the main road (care required; the junction comes abruptly).

Turn right, then go straight on to a major junction with signs to Paleokastritsa and Kerkira. Here go right (Kerkira) and after a brief climb, the road (a main road, but quiet) runs level towards **Agios Ioannis**. After passing on the right a radio listening station and then **Aqualand**, look on the left for a narrow junction (no signpost). Turn down this road (if you reach Agios Ioannis, you have gone too far, and you can either return to look for it or continue to the next road left to **Afra**, which then will lead you back onto your return road). Go left at two T-junctions, then fork right. You are now on the road by which you ascended from **Gouvia**; return down the steep hill to your starting point.

MOUNTAINBIKE TOUR 3

KANONI - PERAMA - ACHILLION - GASTOURI - KINOPIASTES
AGIOS PROKOPIOS - KOURAMADES - KALAFATIONES
VARIPATADES - PINE FOREST - VIROS - PIKOULATIKA
PERAMA - KANONI (30 KILOMETRES)

PICTURESQUE CENTRAL VILLAGES
AND THE PINE FOREST

Unspoilt villages in the centre of the island are the feature of this trip,
which also passes through a mysterious pine forest. On the little roads
between the pictureque villages, new vistas open at every turn.

START at **Kanoni** at the start of the causeway, or at **Perama**.

If you start at Kanoni, cross the causeway (with care) and ascend the path
to the road. Turn left to reach Perama (busy main road; care required).

At the centre of **Perama**, just before the Alexandros Hotel, take the road
signposted *Katsaratika - Gastouri - Achillion Museum*. It is more or less a
constant climb to Gastouri.

Turn left at **Gastouri** for the **Achillion Palace** (fee for entry). After your
visit, head back the way you came, and go straight on. After the main part
of Gastouri, there is a long downhill, with bends, to a T-junction. Turn left,
go right at the next fork, then right at the next junction, which is
signposted *Kinopiastes*. Just 50 or so metres after taking this road, take a
very narrow road left (with a blue sign to a monastery). But it is
recommended that you visit **Kinopiastes**, a very picturesque village with
several coffee bars, before continuing.

The narrow road which passes the monastery (which you may visit if
open) climbs very steeply (you may have to walk) to **Agios Prokopios**.
After the first houses of the village, take the first turn left. Wind through a
pretty neighbourhood, then turn left by a church. This narrow road runs
through another section of the village. At the next T-junction, turn left,
then go right at the crossroads. Ignore the first turning *(Kastellani)* and

take the second (*Kouramades*). Reaching the centre of **Kouramades**, do not follow the sign which reads *Pelekas 4*. Instead, go sharp right, and climb to **Kalafationes**. Here go left at the crossroads and descend briefly to **Varipatades**, a village with a very narrow and twisting main street.

After Varipatades, the road descends with views on all sides.

After a cement factory, turn right on a gravel road. Go left at a fork, and proceed on gravel and dirt through the **Pine Forest**. Your only deviation is a left fork at a main junction, then you reach asphalt again near Kalafationes. Turn left, descend to cross a valley, then climb to **Viros**. Go straight on at the crossroads, then the road drops to the main road at Vrioni. Turn right and after 200 metres, go straight on at a junction (care required; this section of the road is very busy).

Pass a road on the right signposted *Agios Prokopios*, and after two long bends, you must look *very carefully* for your next turning. It comes on the left immediately after a notice on the right which reads *Achilleus Tours*. The entrance is very narrow and is signposted ΠΙΚΟΥΛΑΤΙΚΑ.

This road leads to the hamlet of **Pikoulatika**. After the hamlet, go straight on, then take the next asphalt road right. This climbs to reach the Perama - Gastouri road; turn left here and return to **Perama** or **Kanoni**.

MOUNTAINBIKE TOUR 4

MESSONGI - BOUKARI - PETRITI - PERIVOLI - MARATHIAS
BEACH - ARGIRADES - KOUSPADES - BOUKARI - MESSONGI
(30 KILOMETRES)

SOUTHERN COAST-TO-COAST
AND GOLDEN BEACH

Visit fishing villages on Corfu's east coast. Cross to a golden beach on the west coast. Return through pretty landscape and traditional villages.

START At the main crossroads in Moraïtika

At the crossroads at **Moraïtika** and take the road towards **Messongi**. Cross the bridge, then turn left at the crossroads. A right bend, and you are on the coast road.

After **Boukari** (Spiros Karidis Restaurant is recommended) the road is dirt to **Petriti**. Keep going along the coast to **Kaliviotis**, where the road heads inland. A short ascent brings you to **Perivoli**.

Turn left at the main road, then follow the signs *'To the Beach'*. Then it is a gentle descent of three kilometres to **Marathias Beach**, where the road ends.

Carry your bike across the beach (no road; make sure you do not get the sticky sand in the gear apparatus), and leave the beach by way of the road which begins at the rear of Mandala Restaurant. Ascend to **Marathias** Village and turn left at the main road. Proceed to **Argirades**.

Now follow the signposted road to Boukari, mainly descending through **Kouspades** to **Boukari**. At the sea, turn left and return along the coast road to **Messongi** and your starting point.

BIBLIOGRAPHY

HISTORY & ARCHAEOLOGY

Old Corfu - History and Culture   Nondas Stamatopoulos
Corfu 1993

The Illustrated History of Corfu   Charles C. Climis
Corfu 1994

Kerkyra - From Nausicaa to Europe   Calliope Preka-Alexandri
Adam Editions 1994

Achillion Palace - History and Tour   George Kritikos and Spiros Poulis
Seven Islands Publishing 1991

CULTURE & TRADITION

Costumes from Corfu, Paxos and the Offshore Isles
Elizabeth-Lulu Theotoki
Municipality of Corfu 1994

Greek Traditional Architecture - Kerkyra   Aphrodite Agoropoulou-Birbilis
Melissa 1984

Play's the Thing - An Anthology of Corfu and Cricket
John Forte

A Kitchen in Corfu   James Chatto and W.L. Martin
Weidenfeld and Nicolson 1987

FLORA & FAUNA

The Concise Flowers of Europe   Oleg Polunin
Oxford University Press 1972

Trees and Bushes of Britain and Europe   Oleg Polunin
Oxford University Press 1976

Medicinal Plants of Greece   George Sfikas
Efstathiades Group 1979

Flowers of Greece and the Aegean   William Taylor - Anthony Huxley
Chatto & Windus 1984

Birds of Britain and Europe   Bertel Braun, Hakan Delin and
Lars Svensson
Hamlyn 1970

GENERAL INTEREST

My Family and Other Animals	Gerald Durrell
Birds, Beasts and Relatives	Gerald Durrell
Garden of the Gods	Gerald Durrell
Prospero's Cell	Lawrence Durrell

In the Footsteps of Lawrence Durrell and Gerald Durrell in Corfu (1935-39)
Hilary Whitton Paipeti
Hermes Press & Production 1998

See Corfu and the Ionians
Paul Watkins
Format Books 1990

Corfu - The Garden Isle
S.L. Flamburiari
John Murray 1994

A Heart's Odyssey
Neil Macvicar
Michael Russell 1990

INDEX

Places (towns, villages, neighbourhoods and major sights) encountered on walks and mountainbike tours have been included in this list, with the walk (W) number and the mountainbike (MTB) tour number to indicate on which trip it will be found.

Makrades W15
Marathias MTB4
Messongi MTB4
Mon Repos W2

New Fortress W1
New Port W1
Nissaki W21

Old Fortress W1
Old Perithia W22
Old Port W1
Old Sinies W21

Palace of Saints Michael & George W1
Palaiopolis W2
Paleokastritsa W14
Pantokrator (W17), W21
Perama W3, MTB3
Perithia MTB1
Perivoli MTB4
Petalia W22, MTB1
Petriti MTB4
Pikoulatika MTB3
Platanos W7
Pyrgi MTB1

Roda W16
Rou W21

San Rocco W1, W2
Sfakera W16
Sgourades MTB1

Sokraki W23, MTB1
Solomos Museum W1
Spartilas W23, MTB1
Stavros W8, W9, W10
Stratia W2
Strinilas W17, MTB1
Strongili W10

Templboni MTB2

Varipatades MTB3
Vatonies W14
Vatos MTB2
Viglatsouri W21
Viros MTB3
Vlacherna W3, MTB3

Zigos W23, MTB1

NOTES